MY SHENANDOAH

"Doubtless there is a providence, some special planetary influence for the express purpose of protecting youth from the consequences of its own folly. I can think of no other reason why I am now able to write the story of our voyage."

—Errol Flynn, from *Beam Ends*, 1937

MY SHENANDOAH

The Story of
Captain Robert S. Douglas
and
His Schooner

DOUGLAS CABRAL

TILBURY HOUSE PUBLISHERS

Tilbury House Publishers
Thomaston, Maine

Library of Congress Control Number: 2022936130

Cover and interior design by Frame25 Productions
Printing and binding by Versa Press, East Peoria, Illinois

10 9 8 7 6 5 4 3 2 1

Contents

Author's Note

I am not an unbiased biographer. I have known Robert Douglas since the spring of 1965, when I was working at a Fairhaven, Massachusetts shipyard that hauled *Shenandoah* for annual maintenance. I saw her and immediately climbed the ladder and asked him for a job as deckhand. Later that summer he asked me to fill in for a few weeks in a slot vacated by a hand who had to leave early. In 1970 he hired me as a carpenter to do maintenance work on his schooner *Alabama*—a great mistake on his part. I was a terrible ship carpenter, but I carried on for two years before moving on to a job that better matched my skill set. I have made my home on Martha's Vineyard ever since.

Bob and Charlene and my first wife and I were next-door neighbors in Vineyard Haven for several years. When they went to a Boston hospital to await the birth of their son Jamie, they left their first-born, Robbie, a year and a few months old, with us.

My friendship with Bob and Charlene has sailed along uninterrupted, as has his ardent partnership with what he called, in an abandoned 2014 attempt at a memoir, "the story of my *Shenandoah*." My two sons served on *Shenandoah* and have become wooden-boat sailors themselves. My son Matthew, from my first marriage, is nearly eleven years older than my second son, Christian, so Bob, taking liberty with the definition of a generation, likes to say that ours is the only family from which three generations have served aboard *Shenandoah*.

I am fond of Bob. I admire him. Some lucky folks serendipitously find themselves acquainted with and influenced by one or two unique people who become a life's touchstones. Bob is such a one for me. So, here, I claim only to have written my friend's story as accurately as possible, and as I have known it.

—DAC

Prologue

TARPAULIN COVE, ON THE south shore of Naushon Island, is a popular southeastern Massachusetts anchorage for yachts of all sorts, though motorboats—20-foot outboards to 60-foot cruisers—predominate these days. Visitors are welcome to swim ashore on the privately owned island and to stroll or picnic along the cove's crescent beach.

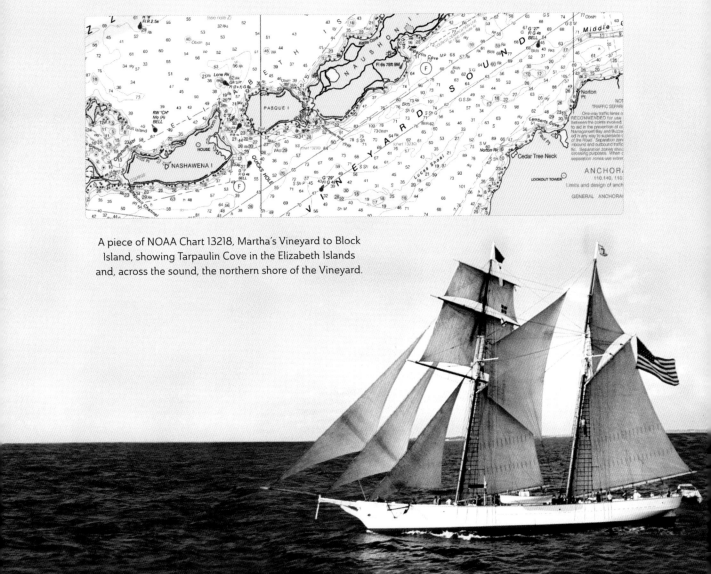

A piece of NOAA Chart 13218, Martha's Vineyard to Block Island, showing Tarpaulin Cove in the Elizabeth Islands and, across the sound, the northern shore of the Vineyard.

The anchorage is open to the east and southeast, facing Martha's Vineyard across Vineyard Sound, but sailors appreciate its spaciousness, ease of access, good holding ground, and deep water near shore. On a summer weekend the cove bustles with strenuous and unrelenting relaxation. But the cove today, on a breezy summer morning in the twenty-first century, is not what Captain Robert S. Douglas imagined in 1964 when he launched the topsail schooner *Shenandoah*, or in 1961 when the sea dream that was to command more than half a century of his life began to take shape.

Captain Douglas does not generally see what you see. He sees more and sometimes less, or rather he sees what commands his interest. When *Shenandoah*, his creation and his alone, enters Tarpaulin Cove, her mere presence transforms this boisterous getaway for modern boaters to a moment in time past, where Douglas lives.

In the eighteenth century, the cove was an anchorage for British warships and for the colonial mischief-makers who dedicated themselves to bedeviling the Royal Navy and

Photographer Nancy Safford took this picture in the early fall of 1968. She had been invited to spend a week aboard *Shenandoah*, shown here at anchor in Tarpaulin Cove. The horses and riders—members and guests of the Forbes families, owners of several of the Elizabeth Islands—were participating in an annual "sheeping," during which riders spread across Naushon Island, the largest in the archipelago, to drive sheep to the farm headquarters for shearing, care, or sale.

the privateers holding letters of marque from King George to target colonial shipping. Unlicensed pirates were frequent visitors, too.

After the colonies shed their Royal oppressors, a steady stream of coastwise schooners running between Maine, Boston, New York, and dozens of ports along the East Coast and in the Caribbean anchored in Tarpaulin Cove to wait for the weather to turn or the current to change in Nantucket and Vineyard sounds. A lighthouse built in 1759, a National Historic Site today, marked the western head of the cove and helped guide coastwise schooner captains. Sailors visited the Cove House for a chat and grog and left messages or mail there for fellow travelers. The Cape Cod Canal (opened in 1914) and the growth of the trucking industry contributed to the weakening and eventual collapse of the coastwise schooner trade. The Boston Seaman's Friend Society cared for mariners at the Cove House until schooner traffic diminished and the Bethel House at Vineyard Haven took on the work of attending to mariners' needs.

In 1961, as he approached his thirties infatuated with the maritime history of the eighteenth and nineteenth centuries, Robert Douglas, the Illinois son of a Republican lawyer and advisor to presidents, suddenly and surprisingly set his course unwaveringly, obsessively, for a berth of his own in this stern and colorful seagoing world in which he had steeped himself and, in a sense, where he would make his life. The grace with which *Shenandoah* rides at anchor in the photograph opposite—no illusion, no computer-graphics trickery needed in any image of her—testifies to the authority of Douglas's unique and resolute vision, so compelling and so influential that most of those who have sailed in her, young and old, crew and guests, bear today the indelible mark of the matchless charms, the rigors, and the lessons learned aboard one man's time-shifting creation.

Chapter One

A Trick at the Wheel

ROBERT DOUGLAS DOES NOT possess an introspective nature. He obsesses, he analyzes, he remembers and plans, but he does not fret over his feelings. Which is not to say that he is dispassionate. On the contrary, he is moved by consuming passions, not a host of them but a few to which he is supremely devoted. One of them, assuredly, is the sailing vessel he calls "my *Shenandoah*." In his 1964 appeal to the Coast Guard in pursuit of a license to operate *Shenandoah* as a passenger vessel, he called the schooner his "life's work for the next fifty years." A faithful description of that life's work will begin best on a typical summer Monday morning between 1965 and 2019.

Shenandoah's practice is to conclude a week's voyage on Saturday, late morning or early afternoon. In the early years, passengers concluding their week's cruise would be put ashore in the schooner's yawl boat or in a Whitehall pulling boat. Starting in the mid-1980s, however, she might disembark passengers via the Vineyard Haven harbor launch or tie up to the Coastwise Packet Company wharf so passengers can step ashore from her deck.

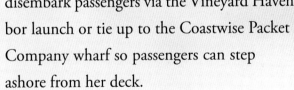

Saturdays and Sundays are devoted to cabin cleanup, laundry, bunk-making, touch-up painting or varnishing, maintenance of the yawl boat engine, sail and rigging repair, and getting the coal for the cookstove on board. On Sunday evening the new week's guests arrive and are put aboard to get settled. Captain Douglas will join them Sunday evening in *Shenandoah*'s main saloon—at the varnished, gimbaled tables in the warm light of meticulously tended kerosene lamps—to welcome his guests and describe what lies ahead.

It is the weekend between trips. Douglas stands in *Shenandoah*'s yawl boat with a member of his crew, puttying and painting, two tasks in the endless slate of chores that he and his hands tackled whenever she was not underway.

Monday is departure day. Stores come aboard, the cook makes breakfast for all and supervises the stowage of the grub. Generally the impatience to set sail builds more quickly than the wind, among passengers—When do we get underway?—and crew—What is he waiting for? The latter gather forward at the fo'c's'le companionway, wondering what goes on in the captain's head, analyzing the passengers, hesitantly mixing with them and telling them what this line does, or that one, and explaining that no, there is no hot water, only fresh water from the hand pumps on deck, and yes, there are two heads down below, one to starboard and one to port. Feel free. A few passengers will ask to go ashore to buy a sweater or maybe a comforting bottle of booze they think they might require.

The crew knows that the wind almost never gets up until late morning or early afternoon, but on this Monday, for no reason except impatience, they think the centuries-old pattern may have changed. For something to do—and because it will have to be done at some point, and maybe doing it now will send a hurry-up message to the captain—the crew runs out a yellow line to the mooring ball to replace the port anchor chain, which will be refastened to the heavier port anchor when *Shenandoah* gets underway.

The captain is not on board. He is raking or sweeping the brick walk in front of the Black Dog Tavern, which sits on the beach sand at the landward end of the Coastwise Packet Company dock. He may even rake the beach itself, which has accumulated some trash. He may chat with a friend or a passenger, but he doesn't stop raking. He may go

A brick walk leads guests to the Black Dog Tavern door. Beyond the tavern lie the beach, the dock, and Vineyard Haven Harbor.

A recent view through the tavern windows—festooned with holiday greenery—
across the beach sand to the Coastwise Packet Company dock.

to his shop, a few steps from the beach, perhaps to find just the right screws with which to install in his cabin some ancient photograph of a schooner he found and admires. It gets to be 11 a.m., then noon. If the breeze is onshore, you can hear the bell ring on the schooner to announce lunch, which is set out on the deckhouse aft. The mate might run the yawl boat ashore, thinking maybe the time has come at last. If it hasn't, he waits at the dock, watching Douglas rake.

Finally, close to 1 p.m., Douglas walks out on the dock, jumps into the yawl boat, starts the engine, takes the tiller, and without a word to the mate, begins the week's trip.

If *Shenandoah*'s chanteyman, Bill Shustik, is aboard for the week, he will take his place before the mainmast, and as the crew and the passengers grasp the thick halyards they hear "Ready on the throat" and then "Ready on the peak," and it is time for everyone—man, woman, and child—to haul away to raise the mainsail. Shustik's voice, diminishing as *Shenandoah* leaves Vineyard Haven Harbor in her wake, can be heard by folks ashore singing, *"Cape Cod girls ain't got no combs/ Haul away, haul away/ They brush their hair with codfish bones/ And we're bound away for Australia/ So heave away, me bully, bully boys . . . / Haul away, haul away . . . ."*

The weekly routine of these halcyon summers had a prequel, of course. Every good story does. *Shenandoah*'s prequel includes 1964, her first year of operation. She sailed that grim summer with guests, not paying passengers, while Douglas went several rounds with the Coast Guard in the struggle to get an operating license. The Black Dog Tavern and the Coastwise Packet Company did not yet exist. The future was unknowable. What was he thinking all those years ago, in June 1965, when he got sail on and left Vineyard Haven for the first time with paying passengers on board, each of them his responsibility and his alone?

"Oh, I don't know. I was just a kid. I really was," he says. "But it was a chance to do a lot of stuff I never could have done otherwise. I tend to look back, and I operated the vessel in ways I wouldn't do now. I'd beat up into Newport in a dark black night against a northeast wind. I'd never do that now.

"My reference point was so different back then. I hadn't been around the boat at all. It was a brand-new boat, and I was a young whippersnapper. Well, I never got into trouble on the boat. We had this fixation to get ahead, get to Mystic if it was possible. A lot of times I'd get down there on a south-

Captain Bob Douglas in his customary place at *Shenandoah*'s wheel. Aloft, a crewman makes his way over the crosstrees and down to the deck after setting the main gaff topsail.

west wind. The southwest winds were just a machine. Push a button, southwest wind, twelve to fifteen. I'd beat down, get into Newport late on Monday night. I couldn't do it unless I had a fair tide in Vineyard Sound. That's twelve miles dead to weather in the sound on Monday afternoon, and you need the tide in your favor. And from Newport it was like thirty miles on the wind to get to Block Island on Tuesday; getting in and out of New Harbor there with a southwest wind was easy, lots of room to anchor.

"If the wind was too far to the west on Wednesday, I couldn't get through Watch Hill Passage; I'd have to stay in Block Island Sound, south of Fishers Island. So I would beat down around the west end of Fishers, and from there I could run up into the Mystic River. If the wind was a little south of west, I could make it. I'd usually get there when it was going dark. I had this fixation to get to Mystic. In the summer of 1968—I've got a logbook to prove it—I was in Mystic every other Wednesday night for six weeks. The alternating weeks I'd head east instead of west out of Vineyard Haven and be in Nantucket on Monday night.

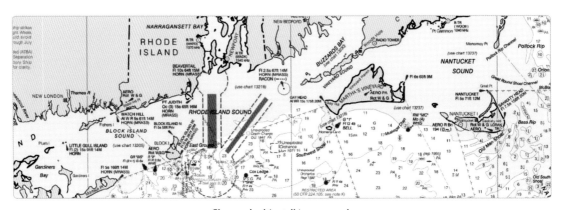

Shenandoah's stalking ground.

"Sailing up the Mystic River was a dumb thing to do. I didn't do it unless the conditions were just right—I *couldn't* do it unless the wind was southeast. You can't get up there under sail with a southwesterly; there are too many buildings up beyond the river, and with high land away from the waterfront areas, you don't get any wind on the water. Often we'd run out of a southwesterly before we even got to the river, but we had to keep going. No problem putting the yawl boat in the water—that's what it's for. But I sailed up that river maybe half a dozen times over the years.

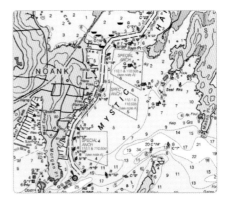

The Mystic River channel, with the Mystic Seaport upriver to the north and Fishers Island offshore to the south—a challenge for a big schooner under sail.

"I didn't have many complaints. The mates were all good guys. I always told my mates, 'I'm giving you my greatest accolade. I'm making you my chief mate.' And that made a big difference who I got. I only fired one mate. He was mate for a couple of summers. We were beating down Buzzards Bay, and I was doing something with another boat, and I told him, 'Brace 'em up sharp,' and he said, 'No, I won't.' I said,

Getting the anchor. Tom Reynolds, the mate, is supervising at right. Charlene Douglas's brother Almy Lapointe, at left, mans one of the windlass bars. Chanteyman Bill Shustik, wearing a Union soldier's cap, sets the hoisting rhythm with a song.

'What?' He said, 'No, I won't.' And so we didn't, and when we got home that weekend, I fired him off the boat. One other mate quit in the middle of the season. Otherwise, they were all good.

"I had my brushes with officialdom over the years. Mystic Seaport, for example. I would call up to say I was heading up the river, and the head waterfront guy at the Seaport would send two of his troops down to Noank in their khaki uniforms to yell from the town dock and the inlet, 'There's no room for you at the Seaport.' I'd go right up there anyway and pull up to *Brilliant*'s dock. Nobody there. Adrian Lane, skipper of the Seaport's schooner *Brilliant*, was a champ. He was a wonderful guy.

"One time we were anchored off Menemsha and a Coast Guardsman at the dock said, 'Where's your running lights?' We didn't have running lights on the yawl boat because there was no place to put them, you know. 'If you don't have them the next time you come in here, I'm going to write you up,' he said, or something like that. And so Adrian, who was on board, had his Coast Guard uniform with him. He took the running lights off *Shenandoah* and set them in the yawl boat on the engine box, and they're so big you could hardly reach around them. And Adrian put on his jacket and his cap—I think he was a Coast Guard captain—and operated the yawl boat. And the Coast Guard guy couldn't say a word."

Through the 1960s, Douglas's "major enterprise for the rest of my life" rewarded him for his idea, his determination, his skillful execution, and his quiet daring. Un-*Shenandoah*

America, meanwhile, convulsed coast to coast in the "free love" decade, which of course was also a decade of vicious national, even global, disharmony—the Vietnam War, the Civil Rights movement, the old-young divide—when, speaking metaphorically, the old were kicked to the curb and the young reckoned they had discovered all the answers that would ultimately matter. "Never trust anyone over thirty," came the word from the Free Speech Movement at the University of California, Berkeley, in 1964, the year *Shenandoah* was launched. Bob was thirty-two that year.

Douglas and *Shenandoah* paid the whole mess little notice. He was not the offspring of bohemian freethinkers and was not a hippie himself—though many of his Vineyard friends and admirers surely fit that mold—nor was he inclined to follow any herd, hip or fogeyish. *Shenandoah* was a gleaming, engineless, floating artifact of times that were receding quickly into the murk of history, at least in the nation's popular conceit. Nevertheless, every summer was a summer of love for Douglas as he delightedly sailed *Shenandoah* up and down the southern New England coast.

A rare occasion. *Shenandoah* finds herself with little wind, and what there is of it is forward of the beam. Every sail in her inventory is set, including the rarely seen fisherman's staysail, which can be a big help in a reaching breeze.

A nearly windless day, and a *Shenandoah* crewman, aloft on the tops'l yard, overhauls the lines that control the square sail to be sure nothing interferes with the set of the sails.

In 1967, Douglas added a second schooner, the 92-foot Thomas McManus – designed *Alabama*, to his fleet. She was a fishing schooner type—think of the 1937 film *Captains Courageous*, starring Spencer Tracy—although she had served throughout her working life as a pilot vessel in Mobile, Alabama. She was fully powered, with only a riding rig for stability. Still, McManus was the dean of fishing schooner designers, something Douglas understood.

In 1970, Douglas's Vineyard friend, the builder Allan Miller, built the Black Dog Tavern of yellow pine timbers from the razed Salem Power Plant in Salem, Massachusetts. Douglas had bought the framing stock with a restaurant vaguely in mind. Set on piers, as a dock would be built, in the sand at the brow of the beach, about 35 feet from the water's edge and next to what is now the office of the Coastwise Packet Company, the Tavern opened in 1971. Douglas said a waterfront town like Vineyard Haven, his adopted home, ought to have a restaurant where sailors could get good chowder and

Christmas approaches, but there is not much room for holiday touches amid the Black Dog Tavern's maritime memorabilia.

spin yarns. It was an instant success and spawned a family retail business with outlets up and down the East Coast.

Douglas decorated the Tavern in his undiluted marine-historical style—each photograph, each painting, each ship's name board, each small-boat transom historic and authentic, all the wooden bits and pieces of long-ago skiffs or schooners found and collected by Douglas himself, and each with a rich backstory he knows and will recite in detail. There are no lobster pot buoys, signal flags, disused lobster pots, or storyless bric-a-brac draped decoratively from the ceiling.

In the 1970s, Douglas got married, had children, and built a tugboat. And later, when the market for week-long sailing cruises for adults weakened and school-age children promised increasingly to be the passengers of the future, he was prepared. He added *Alabama* to his working fleet just when the market developed for the sort of service she could offer. By then, two of his four boys had become skilled mariners themselves, eventually transforming Douglas's Coastwise Packet Company into Black Dog Tall Ships, a family business.

The Coastwise Packet Company dock in the off-season. *Shenandoah* and
Alabama are moored beyond the end of the dock in this foreshortened view.

Only once in the 56 years she was commanded by Captain Douglas, *Shenandoah* anchored
for the night in Fort Pond Bay, Long Island Sound, just west of Montauk Point.

Not even Cassandra, the Trojan priestess of Apollo—despite her out-of-this-world record for farsightedness—could have foreseen any of this in the future of a Midwestern boy who liked horses and thought he might grow up to be a rancher or maybe an airplane pilot, whose mother died when he was very young, and whose father, indispensable advisor to American presidents, spent most of his life in Washington, DC. Douglas's life's work may today seem to have been preordained and assured, but that was hardly the case in his youth or even in 1964, when *Shenandoah* made her maiden voyage.

Chapter Two

Maiden Voyage

"I REALLY DIDN'T KNOW the ins and outs of what was going on. However, it was clear that we left South Bristol after a very cursory check of the navigation system," Dan Goodenough recalled years later. He was a sophomore at Harvard when he signed on as cook on 32-year-old Robert Douglas's newly built schooner *Shenandoah* for her July 1964 maiden voyage from Harvey Gamage's shipyard in South Bristol, Maine, to her homeport on Martha's Vineyard.

Goodenough had worked for three summers as kitchen help and then cook at the Whitehall Inn in Camden, Maine. He was in an architecture class at Harvard with Douglas's younger brother David, who told Goodenough that Robert needed a cook on his new boat. Dan was not a sailor and did not become one. Nor did he become a chef, though he loves to cook and enjoys cooking over a woodfire, as he did on *Shenandoah* for two seasons. Nor did he become an architect. A half-century later he would retire from Harvard Medical School as the Takeda Professor of Cell Biology Emeritus.

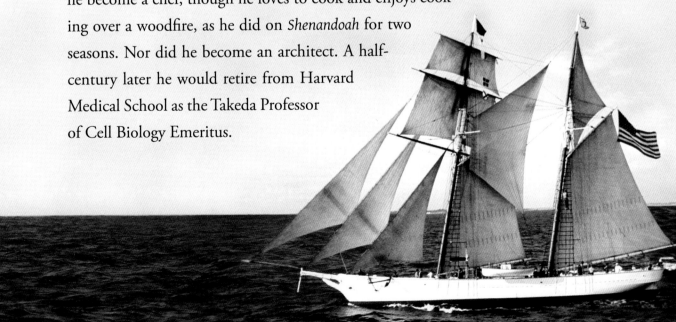

The schooner had been under construction for about a year and three months when she left Gamage's yard, and Douglas had become a fixture in the daily lives of Gamage and his crew. Living in a rented room at the Coveside Inn in nearby Christmas Cove, he was at the yard daily to work with the experienced carpenters and to pester Gamage and his craftsmen toward perfection. At least once, Douglas recalls, the exasperated Gamage complained, "You're too fussy, I can't suit you."

Among the host of tasks unattended when *Shenandoah* departed South Bristol, the compass had not been properly swung. As an interim measure, Douglas had pushed *Shenandoah* off the dock with his yawl boat in company with a friend's lobster boat whose compass had been adjusted; the boats ran parallel courses, comparing compass headings and noting the differences in a deviation table.

Newly launched, *Shenandoah* lies at anchor in the Damariscotta River as her sails are bent on. The fore-sail and mainsail are in place but not yet seized to the booms and gaffs. The square sails, gaff topsail, and jibs have yet to be bent on. The splash of white forward of the foremast may be a kind of primitive ventilator, often called the "ghost," rigged to direct air into the fo'c's'le's close quarters.

"It was also clear that some pretty heavy weather was coming up," Goodenough remembered, "but Bob seemed intent on going. We were supposed to meet with a whole bunch of Sea Scouts in Gloucester, and so we took off. And not long after we got out into the open Atlantic, the weather closed in. It was a classic northeaster. I don't know how it would compare to other northeasters—I'd never been out on the open Atlantic in a boat in a northeaster before—but it was clear that this was quite a storm." Douglas estimates that the gale blew 40 knots or more.

Shenandoah was launched in February 1964, but it was July before she was ready to begin her maiden voyage to Martha's Vineyard. Here she is sailing in company with the Maine windjammer *Mary Day*, Captain Havilah Hawkins, before leaving Maine. None of her three yards is in place, and her main gaff topsail is not set.

Douglas had sailed and raced small sailboats. He had sailed as crew aboard some of the Camden, Maine, windjammer fleet. He owned and had lived aboard *Ayuthia*, a 48-foot centerboard ketch drawn by the English designer Maurice Griffiths and built of teak in Thailand in 1936. Fastened with copper rivets, her bottom copper sheathed, and with a gaff-rigged main and mizzen, she was no modern creation; she was lovely, solid, traditional, meticulously crafted, and certain to appeal to someone who found inspiration in his obsessive study of marine history and sailing craft.

Douglas's sea experience in square riggers, however, was limited to the three months he had spent as a crewman—along with Marlon Brando and Trevor Howard—on the HMS *Bounty* replica used in the 1962 filming off Tahiti of the tale of the eighteenth-century mutiny that overthrew Captain William Bligh. The movie-version *Bounty* departed Lunenburg, Nova Scotia on October 26, 1960, passed through the Panama Canal, and arrived in Tahiti in December. By mid-January 1961, Douglas was back at his parents' home in Washington, DC, his brief movie career behind him. The movie-version *Bounty* was hardly an accurate replica of her historic namesake, powered as she was by twin diesel engines and generators and air conditioned throughout. Her captain was a Nova Scotian, the highly regarded Ellsworth T. Coggins, then 46.

Besides Douglas, only William Bunting, his 17-year-old bosun, could claim service in a square rigger. Bunting had sailed as a student in the brigantine school ship *Albatross,* signing on at the age of 14. The *Albatross* had set a course, upper and lower topsails, and a topgallant on the foremast. Battered by a vicious squall, she capsized and sank within minutes in the Caribbean, about 160 miles west of Key West, on May 2, 1961. Below at the time, Bunting survived by crawling through a dumbwaiter shaft from the main cabin to the on-deck galley and the ocean's surface. The shaft of the dumbwaiter, with *Albatross* on her beam ends and quickly filling with seawater, was nearly horizontal.

Apart from Bunting and Douglas, none of *Shenandoah*'s crew had ever served on a square-rigged vessel, much less conceived, commissioned, and commanded one as Douglas had. Indeed, none had served on a vessel of the size and complexity of the engineless *Shenandoah.* One of them was Douglas's brother John Bruce, younger than Bob by six years. He and Bob had sailed together in Vineyard Haven and on *Ayuthia* in the Bahamas. John had been drafted into the Army, drove trucks during his service, and was discharged in 1963. He had lived in Bob's Vineyard Haven house while Bob lived mostly in Maine during *Shenandoah*'s construction. During his Vineyard summers, John had become a potter, working in a two-story building attached to the cement building his older brother calls his museum. John said that Bob, exercising a common older brother prerogative, often assigned him unappealing sailorly jobs such as going aloft to free a jammed block in the halyard used to set *Shenandoah*'s Christmas tree at the top of the mainmast or going overboard to clear a line that had wrapped itself around *Ayuthia*'s propeller. John went on to become a prolific and prize-winning filmmaker and cinematographer, living most of his life in Vermont.

With luck and a southwest wind, the trip of about 130 nautical miles from South Bristol to Martha's Vineyard might take 24 or 30 hours. For a vessel the size of *Shenandoah,* with her considerable sail area, if the wind were moderate and had more east than west in it, the trip could be shorter. For Douglas and his crew, however, the weather had determined to put them to a daunting test.

"At one point I remember poking my head up through the companionway from the galley where I was trying to prepare food for people," Goodenough remembered. "I watched the bow of the vessel go completely underwater, coming down off a wave, and the bow then scooped up, literally scooped up green water. And as the bow rose, this wave of water came back aft. I just got myself back into the galley in time before all that

Top: Mary Day's yawl boat prepares to push *Shenandoah* off the Gamage Shipyard dock.
Above: Shenandoah gets underway for her Vineyard home.

water came into the galley. It was quite a scene. I didn't get seasick, but it was—I was very interested in keeping my head above deck as much as I could.

"I had prepared a tuna casserole for the crew to eat, but when I set it on the counter, I didn't know enough to secure it properly. There was a pass-through between the galley and the main saloon where guests ate at two long, varnished, gimbaled tables. There was also a gorgeous old pump organ there, and my casserole got thrown through the pass-through and smashed into the pump organ. The poor crew was cleaning tuna casserole off this pump organ for god knows how long after we finally got into port."

Shenandoah, 101 feet long at the waterline, had lingered at Harvey Gamage's South Bristol, Maine dock for several months after her February 15 launching. Work had continued through the spring on the interior accommodations, the deck structures, and myriad

Outer, inner, and jumbo jibs set, along with the main- and foresails and the main gaff topsail, *Shenandoah* hurries from South Bristol to meet a rising northeasterly wind.

other complicated details that Douglas wanted done just so. And there was the lofty rig to assemble and put in place: masts; topmasts; lower, topsail, and topgallant yards; jibboom; and bowsprit. There were shrouds and ratlines to be rigged so the crew could get aloft; halyards, clewlines, buntlines, and leech lines to manage the square sails and the main and foresails; footropes for the crew working aloft on the yards; and downhauls, lifts, halyards, sheets, deadeyes, lanyards, stoppers, and more. Henry Bohndell, a fourth-generation rigger in Rockport, Maine, was responsible for all of the standing rigging.

Although her inspiration was at least partly the result of Douglas's friendships with and study of the captains of the Camden windjammer fleet and their business practices, those passenger vessels were fore-and-aft-rigged schooners and were smaller—about 70 to 90 feet—the exceptions being the 120-foot *Adventure* and the even-larger three-masted *Victory Chimes*. The Maine windjammers were modeled after and indeed, in most cases, had worked their youthful lives as coasting freighters. The Down East freight schooners had traded lumber, ice, coal, kerosene, cordwood, and other cargoes at ports up and down the East Coast in the nineteenth and early twentieth centuries before that trade petered out. Many had centerboards, allowing them to make their way upriver to remote Maine villages, and all of them were designed to be managed by a small crew.

Adapted to carry passengers, the Down East windjammer schooners of the mid-twentieth century attracted sufficient visitors to finance successful businesses, but they required considerable updating and diligent maintenance. They were often run as family businesses: The husband served as captain and chief caretaker; his wife did the cooking and some of the maintenance; and the mate might be one of the couple's children or a college kid free for the summer. The Maine schooners carried perhaps 5,000 square feet of sail. With their shorter rigs requiring fewer hands, they were much simpler and more economical to operate than larger vessels. They exemplified a refined, even elegant model of efficiency—low buy-in, low payroll, hard work—that made their business success possible on a modest but still satisfying scale. A passenger schooner in Penobscot Bay in the latter half of the twentieth century had no topmasts from which to set gaff topsails. None set square sails, and none measured 152 feet from the end of the bowsprit to the end of the main boom as *Shenandoah* did. Planning his schooner, Douglas had immersed himself in the experiences of his predecessors and their businesses, but his conception differed significantly from theirs. The Maine windjammers were in business; Douglas was in thrall.

Shenandoah's masts reach 94 feet above the water. She sets outer, inner, and jumbo jibs, a foresail and mainsail, a fore topsail and fore topgallant on three yards crossing the foremast, and a main gaff topsail besides. Her total sail area is 6,400 square feet without the fisherman staysail. Douglas's plan was to carry passengers on weekly excursions, as the Camden fleet did, but in a vessel with nine paid hands including himself, more dramatic underway, hardly less so at anchor, more challenging to command, and, with her raked masts, descended from a more swashbuckling historic pedigree. Most important, *Shenandoah* was to do her business in southern New England, between Long Island and Nantucket sounds, where in 1964 there were no operating businesses resembling the Maine windjammer fleet, though several would follow in Douglas's wake.

Douglas liked his chances for success, because his home waters featured an abundance of charming and historic anchorages, a fairly dependable sailing breeze, a scarcity of fog, and proximity to prosperous communities from Nantucket to New York and Washington, DC. It is certain he never wrote a detailed business plan—he was, after all, busy altering in several ways the original design of the mid-nineteenth-century vessel that was his inspiration, drawing her modified lines himself, calculating the offsets needed to loft the vessel, drafting her construction drawings, designing her rig and accommodations, and assembling all the gear, from anchors to yawl boats, that she would require. Her homeport was to be Douglas's own adopted hometown at Vineyard Haven on the island of Martha's Vineyard, four miles from the Massachusetts mainland.

Tony Higgins lives on Martha's Vineyard with his wife, Abigail, whose family had long been Vineyard summer residents. Higgins credits Douglas with introducing him to the Vineyard, to his wife whose family summered there, and on one evening in Camden, Maine, to William Bunting, who would become a lifelong friend. That was the evening Higgins and Douglas heard from Bunting the harrowing tale of the sinking of the *Albatross* in the Gulf of Mexico. Higgins became *Shenandoah's* first mate, and Bunting, her bosun.

"That first summer, we were all learning how to sail a schooner. I mean none of us knew a damned thing," Higgins said. "Including Bob. It was a whole lot of shaking down that went on that summer. In fact, the maiden voyage was absolutely hair-raising."

It was a clear, bright day when *Shenandoah* departed South Bristol with a 15- to 20-knot breeze. "Everything was way behind schedule," Higgins recalled, "and when we finally left the Gamage yard it was well into the summer. And we went right out into a northeast blow, and we were tearing along. I mean, we were off the land, but it was a

July 13, 1964. On *Shenandoah's* maiden voyage, she stopped in Gloucester, Massachusetts, to collect a group of Sea Scouts, the first charter group to sail aboard the new schooner. The trip from Maine had been a stern test of *Shenandoah's* seaworthiness. Douglas took a moment for a satisfying row around his proud new command.

hair-raising night, and she was over-canvassed, and we didn't reduce much, and we were dragging the lee rail in the water. The Whitehall boats were floating in their davits, and the compass had yet to be fully adjusted.

"The next morning things cleared up after a vicious night, and we were clueless about where we were. So we just headed west and came in on Cape Ann and the two towers, the two lighthouses there, and then we knew where we were."

Jeremiah Goodale, a Martha's Vineyard teenager, spent a month in South Bristol working twelve-hour days with his fellow crewmen to get the schooner rigged before *Shenandoah* left for Martha's Vineyard. He remembers that maiden voyage this way: "Well, first of all, we spent about—oh, the whole month of June, beginning of July— rigging her in South Bristol. Then we finally headed out, and at night it came on to blow hard northeast. Everything was set except the topgallant, and it would have been set too except that it hadn't been rigged before we left. And we stretched the living hell out of the rigging, because all the rigging was new and was trying to get seated, even though we had tightened up the shrouds as best we could. We spent the whole damned night con-

tinuing to tighten the shrouds and driving the wedges down around the masts, because the masts were moving and trying to spit the wedges out. So we finally got down off Glouces-ter and spent the rest of the night tacking back and forth, waiting to go in at daylight."

"We went into Gloucester, unbent the main and foresail, and took them to a sailmaker," said Higgins. "We took two feet off the head of the main and two feet off the fore,

The *James J. Minot*, all decked out for carrying passengers on tours of the Boston Harbor islands. Robert's brother David owned the *Minot*, a 50-foot, diesel-powered general-purpose workboat, when *Shenandoah* was launched, and met the schooner at the east end of the Cape Cod Canal.

because we had used these brand-new canvas sails and stretched them all out. So anyway, we got all that fixed and then finally made it down to Woods Hole. It was a learning experi-ence that summer."

Unlike Higgins and Goodale, Douglas remembers taking in sail and getting down to four lowers as the gale strengthened. Either way, Shenandoah's maiden voyage was a stern test.

From Gloucester, *Shenandoah* made her way under sail to the eastern end of the Cape Cod Canal, where she was taken in tow by Douglas's brother David in his 50-foot wooden workboat *James J. Minot*. Douglas's friends Skippy Ritter and the beloved Chan-dler Moore, an off-and-on resident of Douglas's Vineyard Haven house, were the tow-boat crew. The *Minot* had operated as a tugboat in Boston and as a licensed passenger vessel. Owned by the city—or perhaps, in what would certainly have been an unusual arrangement, by the city and Boston Mayor James M. Curley in partnership—she was used for excursions to the Boston Harbor islands for the mayor's constituents. Douglas later traded his Crosby catboat *Dover* for the *Minot* and owned the towboat for 12 years.

"I didn't really need him," Douglas said of the passage through the canal. "I got a breeze." But what breeze there was was on the nose, and anyway canal rules require all vessels to be under power or tow.

Shenandoah anchored in Great Harbor, Woods Hole, Massachusetts, where a small crowd greeted the newcomer. One of the welcoming friends, Woods Hole – based dock builder Dan Clark, asked Douglas if there was anything he needed. Douglas said he badly needed a ride to Logan Airport. Clark pointed to his old Dodge sedan and said, "Hop in." Douglas was in a hurry to attend the first hearing for his appeal of the US Coast Guard's refusal to license *Shenandoah* to carry paying passengers. The hearing was to begin the next day in Washington, DC.

What was to have been a triumphant season—*Shenandoah*'s first summer in business and under sail—was instead laced with disappointment and hounded by the distinct possibility that Douglas's great conception might be alto-

Douglas stands on the wheelbox while steering his 28-foot Crosby racing catboat *Dover* out of Vineyard Haven Harbor. Bob traded *Dover* to his brother for *Minot,* which served as *Shenandoah's* towboat and tender for 12 years.

gether ruined. The Coast Guard's refusal to license *Shenandoah* to carry passengers that summer meant that all the 1964 passengers got their deposits back and sailed for free, while Douglas immersed himself in a year-long appeal of the Coast Guard's decision. He would have ample opportunity in that long year to ask himself how a Midwestern kid who had grown up riding horses and flying planes had ended up as the captain of a ship without a license.

Chapter Three

A Midwestern Boy

ROBERT STUART DOUGLAS was born on March 18, 1932, in Chicago's St. Luke's Hospital, to James Henderson Douglas Jr. and Grace Farwell Douglas. He grew up in Lake Forest, Illinois. James Douglas, whose father had been a founder and vice president of the Quaker Oats Company, was born in Cedar Rapids, Iowa, in 1899. He had been commissioned as a second lieutenant in the Army while a Princeton student in 1918, but had not served overseas in World War I. He became a lawyer and investment banker.

Six months after Robert's birth and three years into the Great Depression, James accepted a post as Assistant Secretary of the Treasury in President Herbert Hoover's administration. He resigned in June 1933, three months into the presidency of Franklin Roosevelt, publicly opposing Roosevelt's New Deal spending plans.

James H. Douglas Jr., Robert's father, sat for this photo in 1960. He was President Eisenhower's Deputy Secretary of Defense at the time.

Robert Douglas's mother, Grace Farwell McGann Douglas, in 1929.

James served again in the armed forces in World War II, rising in rank from major to colonel. He became chief of staff for the Air Transport Command and was awarded the Distinguished Service Medal. In the postwar years he served the administration of President Dwight David Eisenhower as Under Secretary (1953 – 1957) and Secretary (1957 – 1959) of the Air Force and as Deputy Secretary of Defense from January 1960 to the end of Eisenhower's presidency. He was instrumental in the creation and siting of the US Air Force Academy, and in 1960 was awarded the Medal of Freedom by President Eisenhower for his government service.

Robert's mother was born Grace Farwell McGann in Lake Forest, the daughter of Grace Farwell and Robert Greaves McGann. She was the granddaughter of United States Senator Charles B. Farwell and a niece of the composer Reginald De Koven. Her mother's family was prominent in Lake Forest and had played an instrumental role in the layout, design, and construction of the city.

Grace Douglas was nearly six feet tall and beautiful. "She'd come and kiss me goodnight every night, I think. I was only seventeen when she died. Lung cancer. She was a great lady. I never—well, she was my mother, I'm a little opinionated maybe in that area. But she was a fabulous woman. After she died, people I didn't know from Adam said she was wonderful. She was—I don't know how to describe her. She was very special," Douglas says.

Grace married James in 1927 and gave birth to four sons: James Henderson Douglas III, born January 27, 1930; Robert; John Bruce, born July 13, 1938; and David Ogden, born July 6, 1940. Robert and David would both settle on Martha's Vineyard. David died in Florida in 2016. James lived most of his life in Paris, until Robert and Charlene

Douglas flew there to bring him back to their Vineyard Haven home for end-of-life care. He died April 6, 2018, at the Martha's Vineyard Hospital in Oak Bluffs. The fourth son, John Bruce, lived in Burlington, Vermont until his death in January 2022.

John described his brother Bob as "inward, nervous as a kid. He was the one who didn't want to go to the party."

The Lake Forest house on the shore of Lake Michigan that Robert grew up in.

Bob got his first taste of life under sail in the summer of his eighth year at Camp Knowsley in Shelby, Michigan. Camp Knowsley offered sailing adventures on Round Pond in four 10-foot, spoon-bowed catboats. Students had to be able to swim, identify the parts of the boat and its rig, get sail on, cruise the lake, and make it back to the landing in

Left to right: The four brothers: David, John, Robert, and James Douglas.

Robert Douglas became a horse lover at the Russell Ranch School in the 1940s. Decades later, in the mid-1970s, he competed in the impromptu races held annually in a field at the West Tisbury farm of Katherine Hall and Ben Reeve, riding his beloved palomino stallion Tipper. Charlene Douglas said her husband nearly won one of the races but came in second behind a mare that Tipper refused to pass.

one piece. Robert did all that, winning himself a sporty captain's hat and the right to take out a boat on his own.

Still, in Robert Douglas's youthful dreams, he did not picture himself as master of a clipper ship running her easting down across the Indian Ocean in the westerly gales of the Roaring Forties or rounding Cape Horn for Asia, Japan, or San Francisco. Instead, his reveries ran to horses. When he was twelve years old, his parents sent him to the Russell Ranch School in Tucson, Arizona, and he spent three pleasant years there in the Sonoran Desert region near the Santa Catalina Mountains. Bob's wife, Charlene Lapointe Douglas, insists that he wanted to be a cowboy, not a ship's captain.

In a 2015 account in the *Oro Valley News,* Heather Nenadovich described the Russell Ranch School as "an Oro Valley legend for those who attended":

> The ranch school movement began in the western United States in the early 1900s as a way to provide education for those families living in remote rural areas. However, it wasn't long before they garnered attention from Easterners who could afford to send their children to boarding school to receive an education based on experiencing nature, the West, and gaining independence that was all the rage. Arizona led the way for national ranch schools, most of which were in the Tucson area, until the movement declined in the 1960s and most were closed.
>
> Rev. Robert Russell, a Presbyterian clergyman from Larchmont, New York, opened Russell Ranch School in 1938. A graduate of Princeton Theological Seminary, he remained the school's headmaster until it closed in 1950. The school has been described as having a main ranch house, a library, craft room, boy's dormitory, several classrooms, and a large corral with horseback riding every day.
>
> Many dignified men have recounted their time spent at the school through interviews and books, including colonels, authors, and at one time, a Rockefeller was said to have attended. I share with you that I too have spent some time on that ranch though it is a bit different now. The dorm rooms have been converted to casitas, the once-library holds storage, and there is a pool to use on the hottest of summer days. I assure you, the sense of history remains strong, and those who have spent time on the ranch have shared in the folklore of stories from the mischievous boys at the school to the "hippie compound" it became in the 1970s.

Many prosperous American parents sent their children to ranch schools, believing that the dry climate was healthy and the ranch work required of the students would strengthen them and encourage confidence and self-reliance. In Douglas's case, the choice of the Russell Ranch was motivated by his health. "I'd had rheumatic fever and spent a month in bed with it, and they thought it would be good to go to stay in a warm spot, I think the story was," he explains.

That Robert Russell had graduated from Princeton, as had James Douglas, probably clarified the choice.

"I was happy," Robert Douglas recalls. "I had a horse." He visited the ranch property in 2004 during a cross-country trip with his wife, but he was sorely disappointed with what he found, "a suburbia of houses as far as you could see."

On a 1988 trip to collect a horse trailer in Cresco, Iowa, Robert and Charlene stopped in Norham, Ontario, Canada, where Douglas's paternal grandfather had been born. "We found the house and talked to people who knew what was going on. Found the grave, which was kind of fun. My grandfather was one of five kids. There's a picture on the wall, five brothers. I think two of them moved to the United States, including James, my grandfather, who was a partner in the Quaker Oats Company, only it was called something else back then, a name I should know but don't. He moved to Cedar Rapids, Iowa, where my father was born, and then they moved to Chicago."

A view of the campus at the Russell Ranch School.

The company that became Quaker Oats was founded in 1901 from the merger of several oat mills, one of which was owned by John Stuart, his son Robert Stuart, and their partner George Douglas, the families from which Captain Robert Stuart Douglas of *Shenandoah* is descended.

In 1947, when Robert Douglas was fifteen, Edward Pulling—like Douglas's father a Princeton

The boys' dormitory at the Russell Ranch School.

graduate, and the founder of the Millbrook School in Millbrook, New York—persuaded James to add himself to the circle of prominent education, literary, military, and government notables who summered on Martha's Vineyard. The family rented a house on West Chop overlooking Vineyard Haven's outer harbor, and Douglas's father later bought it. The house had belonged to Colonel George Goethals, supervisor of the construction of the Panama Canal, and had been moved to its waterfront site by Vineyard carpenter Horace A. Tilton. Robert remains struck by the coincidence that his family's house in Lake Forest had also been moved, intact, about a hundred feet from where it was built to a waterfront site on the shore of Lake Michigan. Both houses were about the same distance from the water's edge, and both faced east.

"I don't know if Dad came down to inspect the place," Douglas says. "I bet he flew in here one weekend in the winter and took a look at houses. I don't think he'd have gone in blind. And the craziest part is, the house in Lake Forest, which is still standing after it was almost torn down and rebuilt in the last few years, faces Lake Michigan, and everything about these two houses is the same. Both are Greek Revival, balusters and porches and the big, heavy cornices. Both were built the same year. Both were moved. Both had a public right-of-way at their north boundary.

"The house in Lake Forest was built out of lumber from the World's Fair Columbian Exposition in Chicago, in 1893, which kind of put a date on it. Dad's Vineyard Haven

Robert and his mother, Grace Farwell Douglas, sailing in the summer of 1947 aboard their 18-foot Menemsha Class sloop *Lucky*. It was Douglas's first summer on Martha's Vineyard. He was 15 years old. Grace, 39 in this photograph, died of lung cancer two years later.

house was built on Crocker Avenue—taking pieces from oak trees was nothing back in those days—and moved up in 1918. Why I remember these things I don't know. Anyway, Dad rented the house, and we had a pretty good time. It was the first time I had anything to do with a real sailboat."

To this day, Douglas has three indispensable requirements for a sailboat he will love, apart from smart wood construction. She must be "knock-down, drag-out beautiful, she must sail like a witch, and she must steer like a dream." The Camp Knowsley catboats had not met the mark—no inspiration there— but that summer Bob, his older brother James, and their mother shared, first, a little Menemsha Class sloop, an 18-footer built at Martha's Vineyard Shipyard, and then a Vineyard Haven 15 named *Wideawake*, number 30 of her racing class, designed and built

A winter image of Douglas's "museum." The entrance to the cement building was enlarged with jack-hammers to squeeze the pilot cutter *Raider* in. The two-story wooden building at the far end of the complex is Douglas's shop and, years earlier, his brother John Douglas's pottery studio.

of wood by Erford Burt, who worked for the Martha's Vineyard Shipyard, then owned by William Colby. "I still have the advertising clipping from the *Vineyard Gazette*: 'For Sale. Vineyard 15. $1,200.' Dad bought the Vineyard Haven 15 for Jim and me that winter," Bob says.

Later Burt operated his own Burt's Boatyard on the shore of Lagoon Pond in Vineyard Haven. He knew precisely what was required of a one-design class of racing sloops for the competition and conditions outside his builder's shed. The Vineyard Haven 15 grew to a class of fifty boats, each 15 feet on the waterline and 21 feet overall, Marconi rigged. The sleek and quick keelboats were designed to stand up to the boisterous breezes common in Vineyard waters in summer. The last of the Fifteens was built in 1970, by then in fiberglass.

A. Bowdoin Van Riper and Katharine P. Van Riper, third- and fourth-generation Fifteen sailors, chronicled the class history in the *Vineyard Gazette* and created the Vineyard Fifteen website. "The older wooden boats simply wore out," they wrote. "The transom of *Panthea* (#11) and a bow timber from *Irish Gal* (#2) are on display in the lobby of the Black Dog Tavern, part of owner Bob Douglas's tribute to the class."

Inside the museum, craft of all sorts, including a Bahama dinghy and a yawl boat, await the call to service.

Douglas still has *Wideawake*, stored in the large cement-clad, longleaf yellow pine – framed building he thinks of as his museum. Among the exhibits there are his racing catboat *Dover*, the 48-foot pilot cutter *Raider* he bought in Ireland (and which is being rejuvenated by Dominic Zachorne, a former *Shenandoah* mate, as this is written), and a herd of skiffs and small boats of a multitude of types, plus lumber, fastenings of all conceivable sizes, and tools. There are two *Shenandoah* yawl boats—so Douglas will have a spare if anything happens to the one hanging in davits at *Shenandoah*'s stern—and countless marine odds and ends he's come across over the years and kept in case he suddenly needs a fitting that isn't manufactured anymore or wants to give something, an anchor or a windlass perhaps, to a friend who has an emergency or is planning to build a boat of which Douglas will be fond.

James H. Douglas III, called Jimmy, was two years older than Robert. The two boys, and sometimes their mother, sailed *Wideawake* for fun and for the Wednesday and Saturday races. "It didn't work out too good, I remember," Douglas admits, "but we survived. About that time Jimmy became a Parisian, so then we didn't see much of him." Douglas and his friend Roy Goff cruised aboard *Wideawake* in the Elizabeth Islands, across

The rehab of the 48-foot pilot cutter *Raider* is a big project but a rewarding one.

Vineyard Sound from Martha's Vineyard. *Wideawake* had no accommodations of any sort, so the boys anchored her each night and slept on the beach.

After three school years in the Southwest, young Robert was sent for five years to the Cate School in Carpinteria, California, graduating in 1951. The school was set on the top of a mesa about three miles from the ocean. Once more, family connections made the Cate School an easy choice. Douglas's mother's family owned a large Spanish-style house overlooking the Channel Islands, and although her father and mother had divorced, Grace Douglas's father, Robert G. McGann, lived there. He and Grace were acquaintances of Curtis Cate, founder of the school, which in 1948 had a student body of about eighty. Curtis Cate "took me under his wing," Douglas says. Many of the students had horses. Cate loaned his horse, Bear, to Douglas, and on weekends Robert rode out from the oceanfront campus with one or two other students into the foothills and the beautiful Valley of the Moon.

The school provided a varied and companionable curriculum. Each evening, the students and faculty gathered to hear Headmaster Cate, seated on one side of the fireplace in the school's meeting room, read aloud while his wife sat knitting on the other side of the hearth. One afternoon each week students devoted themselves to maintenance projects on campus. In his spare time, Douglas built boat models.

Douglas was never a star scholar, but his record at the Cate School included first honors in a contest for selection and recitation of poetry. He chose Matthew Arnold's "Dover Beach," a late-nineteenth-century poem whose speaker stands on the Dover coast looking across the English Channel toward Calais. The poem laments the withering of the Christian faith in England as science commanded the public's interest, and the last stanza resonated with students in the war-weary mid-1940s:

> Ah, love, let us be true
> To one another! for the world, which seems
> To lie before us like a land of dreams,
> So various, so beautiful, so new,
> Hath really neither joy, nor love, nor light,
> Nor certitude, nor peace, nor help for pain;
> And we are here as on a darkling plain
> Swept with confused alarms of struggle and flight,
> Where ignorant armies clash by night.

Douglas's secondary-school record failed to impress the Ivy League admissions officers. "I wasn't too sharp in school," he says. "Of course I applied to Princeton, because Dad had gone to Princeton, but I didn't make it in, and he didn't have enough drag. Now they call it pull. If you had a parent who went there, you had a pretty good chance of getting in yourself. Somehow that didn't work out, but the headmaster of Cate School—the guy who replaced Curtis Cate when he retired—had been dean of admissions at Brown, or at least mixed up with Brown to some extent, and he said, 'If you want to go to Brown, I can get you in no problem.'"

But Bob chose Northwestern University instead. Grace Douglas had died in 1949, and the following year James married Elinor Thompson Donaldson. (He told Robert that he was following Grace's instructions.) Now, Douglas was thinking of his remaining parent. "I hadn't seen much of Dad all my life," he explains. "When I was a kid, he'd get an 8 o'clock train to Chicago every day in the same automobile that would drop me off at school. We saw him on the weekends. Then I was away at school, and he was posted overseas during World War II. I was impressed by him. He spent more time working for his country than he did working for his law firm in Chicago. He must have been impressive to be appointed Assistant Secretary of the Treasury when he was 32 years old.

"So I decided Northwestern was a good stop because it's about 30 miles from Lake Forest, and Dad was at home. I thought, shucks, now I'll get a chance to see my dad. But he got the job with Eisenhower and moved to Georgetown. I sort of screwed up there."

When President Eisenhower asked Douglas's father to join him in Washington, "I remember Dad asked me, 'What the hell should I do? I know you're back going to school here largely because you haven't ever been at school near home. Except grade school.' And I said, 'Oh, shit. I can't imagine you got a job working for Eisenhower in the federal government. You're crazy if you don't take it.' I doubt it made any difference that I said that. But he did take the job, and he wound up being the longest serving officer of Eisenhower's administration. He stayed the full eight years."

Still, Northwestern suited him. "I still think—fondly might not be the right word—of two teachers in particular. I took every class I could get from them. One was an absolute socialist to the core, and the other was Mr. Conservative. [They were Paul Arthur Schilpp and William Montgomery McGovern, respectively. McGovern is said to have been fluent in seventeen languages and may have been the inspiration for the film character Indiana Jones.] I remember they had a dialogue in the university's gym or biggest auditorium. It was loaded with people, but you could have heard a pin drop. They were two exotic guys. McGovern wrote a lot of books. *From Luther to Hitler* was one. An intensely interesting guy. These two guys were fabulous people. Made Northwestern worthwhile. Because how many good teachers do you get in any educational enterprise?"

Douglas did not choose Northwestern course offerings in marine engineering, naval architecture, science, drafting, or mathematics. "You had to take two modern language courses if you didn't take any math. I started off taking a calculus course, and I think that was a week that Dad was still home. I said, 'Dad, you've got to help me with this,' and he didn't have a clue. So I said, 'I'm bowing out of this one.' It was still within the time you could drop a course and pick up another. And you could satisfy the requirements if you took a year of biology and—what's it called—not geography, but a great course. It covered everything you could imagine, from weather charts to topography, maps, I can't remember what else. But you had to work on them."

Douglas did some sailing on the Vineyard during college summers, but he concentrated chiefly on flying. He had been trained by Carolyn Cullen, owner and operator of the Oak Bluffs Airport, a grass field home to Trade Wind Flying Service, now a Martha's Vineyard Land Bank property enjoyed as a dog park. Cullen had trained enlistees at the Naval Air Force at Schenectady, New York, during the first two years of World War II, and then had served in the Women Airforce Service Pilots (WASP) division of the US Army Air Corps. WASP was a civilian women pilots' organization whose members were United States federal civil service employees. Members of WASP tested and ferried aircraft and trained other pilots, freeing male pilots for combat roles in the war. After the war, Cullen was promoted to the rank of captain in the Air Force Reserve. She was the first woman to solo an airplane in Berkshire County, Massachusetts, and she earned her commercial license and instructor's rating and worked as a flight instructor at various airports in the East. By 1947 she owned the airport where, in 1949, at 17, Douglas made his first solo flight in a J3 Piper Cub.

If Bob's grades had not been in the top half of his Northwestern college class, he might have been drafted for the conflict in Korea. Instead he chose four years of Air Force ROTC, and after graduating from Northwestern in 1955, he went to flight school at Lackland Air Force Base in San Antonio, Texas, for preflight training. He had a three-year commitment to serve but not yet a certain future flying jets in the military, though that is where he seemed to be headed.

Douglas liked the Air Force. "I always thought the training was remarkably engineered, and I relate my experience in the Air Force to climbing a ladder, just reaching the next rung, you know? You could just go to the next airplane or next school. They geared it for me perfectly. I never bet any money on the fact that I would get my wings. They would lose about 10 percent of each class to attrition.

"I reported for flight-training duty in January 1956. There were ten primary flying schools, and the Air Force was transitioning them to chartered civilian operation, weeding out the worst ones—or the ones needing the most investment—first. Mine was called Graham Air Force Base because a guy named Graham had taken over the defunct World War II auxiliary field and built whatever was needed in the way of buildings and stuff. The Air Force had a nucleus of folks there wearing the uniform, and the aircraft were all Air Force. By that time Graham was one of the nine civilian-operated flight schools, all of which were far better than the last remaining school run by the Air Force. The Air Force – owned school was the 'sucker school' because the instructors there had only been flying a year and a half, something like that. You'd go through basic and then you'd have to go be an instructor and teach people. In the civilian-owned schools, on the other hand, the pilots were old guys with thousands of hours' experience flying in World War II, like Frank Agnew, my instructor, who became my friend. They were a special crowd of people; you had to be good or you wouldn't be there, you know? And Frank was a beautiful example.

"Graham Air Force Base was in Marianna, Florida. We flew T-34 and T-28 propeller-driven trainers there. Maybe I lucked out, but Frank was a wonderful guy. He came sailing with me forever.

"I had a good time in the Air Force. I still think of flying, but flying, you know, is long periods of boredom interspersed with moments of stark terror. Something like that.

"Later they taught us how to fly a T-33 trainer jet in a tight formation on somebody's wing, because the F-86L that the instructor flew had a swept-back wing that kept you in the perfect location in the formation. Sometimes, if you lost your air speed indicator, it was the difference between throwing your airplane away or bringing it back. By the time you finished flying, maybe half the aircrafts would be written up, out of commission. The planes didn't have very good longevity—they were too complicated. So they had a need to fly on the wing. And we would take off on the instructor's wing.

"When we graduated to the F-86s, you'd have to stand a five-minute alert. Maybe one day a week, something like that. There were alert hangars at the end of the base, and there were always four aircraft plugged in and ready to go—two in each hangar, I think—with your parachute in the seat ready to be strapped on, and your hard hat sitting on top of the windscreen. You'd be up in the flight shack, and the whistle would go off, and you had to take off on the wing and be wheels in the wells in five minutes. And you could do it.

"You had to have pretty good control over that airplane. When you had to recover on the wing, you would be flying in formation with the next F-86, which was nice, because you could stack down with your eyesight on that wing line, looking right down the lead against the wing. That was your locator. Landing at night on the wing was hairy but impressive."

The collision that grounded Douglas for a month destroyed two aircraft. "And I caused it!" he shouts, telling the story. Actually, he did not. At the time he was still flying T-33s out of Greenville Air Force Base in Greenville, Mississippi.

"I used to tell all my friends, after the fact, I said, 'Don't ever get yourself in a frame of mind where you don't want to tell your skipper—and that's your flight instructor—that he's fucking up, doing something really stupid.' That frame of mind caused me to keep my mouth shut in the back seat when my skipper put us all in this situation.

"We came along in our initial landing approach, one thousand feet altitude, which is gear and flaps. Gear down as the plane circles left. Speed brakes, gear, flaps, downwind, be astern, land, okay? So we're on the initial angle about a mile from the end of the runway, a thousand feet up. And there's a guy—four guys actually, an instructor pilot and his students—manning a mobile control tower, a truck with a little house on its back, orange checks on it, you know? These four guys would have been flying from seven in the morning till noon, after which their job was to keep clearance between all aircraft.

"So anyway, my skipper was Joe Colleran, and he was a hot pilot, and he loved to impress. He'd pull a lot of Gs to make you throw up in the back seat, that sort of stuff. So we were killing airspeed real fast. By the time he got downwind on the pattern, he had reached gear- and flap-lowering speed, and he started the base turn. But the guy who was in the pattern before us, who we hit, was by himself, a student, and he came in four Gs, no need to do that. And so he's way out on his base turn. We slow downwind, and just as we start our base turn I remember looking out over the canopy and I could see this other guy coming in way out there, but they should have been on the same track. I see him, but I don't tell the skipper. I've just come back from two hours in the back seat flying instruments, which wrings the shit out of you, and all you really want to do is take a shower and turn in, you know. I should have said something, like 'You idiot, look what you're doing,' or 'Take it around,' or something like that, but I didn't. So we wind up making contact, and the guys on the mobile control say, 'Number Two, take it around,' but this other guy thought he was number two, and he hit us. There was a big boom noise. Joe said he tried to roll the airplane, to keep it flying, but we went into a creek that ran across the approach end of the runway. This was the eighth of January 1957, about one in the afternoon.

"The T-33 was a good, rugged airplane. We figured from the way things looked—it was the height of the rainy season down there, and this little creek with levees was full to the brim—that we hit the full creek at full tide, because at low tide, most likely there wouldn't have been any water in the creek. Anyway, the guys who were in my flight—the squadrons come in two flights, one flying in the morning and the other in the evening—were playing baseball in the backyard of the bachelor officer quarters, and they saw this great shot of water going up quite a way from the BOQ and the runway.

"The impact was somewhat mollified by six, seven, eight feet of water in the creek, but the airplane hit one wing and the impact took the plane apart. The nose, the engine, and the wings were all gone. Just the cockpit section was still in one piece, but we were

This Air Force photograph of the crash scene shows Douglas's T-33 upright in a drainage ditch, which was fortunately full of water and cushioned the crash. He waited some time in his cockpit seat before help arrived.

stuck under a small tree and nose-down at an angle. And there was a tree sticking up there, over the canopy, and the canopy wouldn't open.

"It all worked out pretty good. We had to wait for half an hour or so because the radios in the fire trucks wouldn't communicate with the tower that had seen it happen, so it took them a while to find out where we were. The guy who came was going to chop a hole in the canopy. Certain things you remember. I said, 'Don't chop a hole in the one part of the airplane that's in one piece.' So they chopped the tree down instead, and we swam out. Joe broke an ankle and got cut up on his hands and face a little bit, but nothing bad. I broke my back.

"He was the pilot, so he was judged to be at fault. Well, neither pilot in either aircraft saw the other guy, obviously, so it was both their faults, I guess. But I told him, 'I feel kind of bad that I didn't tell you, because I saw it.'

"I crushed a vertebra and was grounded for a month. That sort of slowed things down. They put me in a full body cast. It was a nuisance."

After a month's sick leave, Douglas returned to Greenville Air Force Base in Mississippi and graduated from basic training there, but not with his original class. Douglas did get back to flying, in advanced training in F-86s from Moody Air Force Base in Valdosta, Georgia, for six or eight months. He was awarded his wings in a ceremony at Greenville. "As I say, I never would have put any money on getting my wings. I certainly

The F-86 Douglas flew when he got his wings. His name, "Second Lieutenant Robert S. Douglas," is visible but not readable below the after end of the canopy.

worked hard. I never worked so hard. But it's easier for some people. Frank Agnew came to Greenville Air Force Base for the ceremony, and Dad said it was one of the happiest days he could remember. He had to be on Capitol Hill—doing something in Congress—so he couldn't make it, but he sent Ross Milton, his exec and a wonderful guy. Ross was 42 then. He had led a bombing raid in the war and come back with half the B-17s he left with. Three hundred were on the raid, and 150 came back. Crazy shit. But what a wonderful guy he was. Anyway, he showed up to give the speech.

I don't remember what he talked about. Of course, the Air Force gives you a set of wings, and I was getting them, and I got Frank Agnew to pin them on. And for some reason or other, Ross Milton was standing right there, and he takes the wings, and says, 'You don't want those. Here.' And he gave me his wings. That was pretty cool.

"Your assignment after getting your wings depended on what slots were in the orders that came down for your graduating class. For my group, single-engine slots were all that were out there. Very democratically, they used gallon pails. Everybody put their ID card into the pail, and the chief would shuffle them around. And the second card he drew was mine. There was one slot for Hanscom Air Force Base in Massachusetts, and I thought, 'Yay, here's my first chance to see New England in the wintertime,' so I took it.

"I had not quite a year at Hanscom, and I had a good chance to check out the area and decided it was a pretty good spot."

And Douglas took every chance he could to spend off-duty days at the house on Martha's Vineyard that his father had bought by then.

But the Air Force had more pilots than it needed in 1958, and pilots were being interviewed and told that they could be released early if they chose. His commanding officer told Douglas he would be making a mistake if he left before his commitment expired. "'This would be a great career for you,' he said. So I said, 'I'll stay,' and I signed up for three more years. But then I'm walking down the hall, back to my flight room, and I said to myself, 'Jesus, are you crazy? They don't want you! Don't you understand? They want you to leave.' So I changed my mind.

"Dad wanted me to stay in, but I said, 'No, Dad. I've tried the twentieth century. Flying a jet aircraft is the most unnatural thing a human being can do. The airplane doesn't want to be up there, and if the fuel runs out, you're coming down. No, I want to get back to the waterfront. I like it there.' So I got out of the Air Force in October 1958 and haven't been in the front seat of an aircraft since. I stayed in my dad's house that winter. It had heat by then. And I bought my downtown Vineyard Haven house a couple of years later. We got the paperwork straightened out while I was in Tahiti, early 1961."

Douglas's own Vineyard house was old, venerable, worn, and comfortable. It sat on a low bluff and was fronted by giant ash trees framing a broad view of Vineyard Haven Inner Harbor, where *Shenandoah* and later *Alabama* would one day lie at their moorings. The house was called Beachside, and it became for years a casually kept bachelor household, with Bob's brother Johnny sometimes in residence, along with a variable cluster of friends, their girlfriends, and later, *Shenandoah* crewmembers. One of the inmates,

A to-do list between two knees on *Raider*'s deck in Bob Douglas's "museum" offers mute testimony to a wooden boat's demands: "Remove old caulking + putty; remove all fastenings; flush out plank edges; fill holes with epoxy + bungs; clean top of keel and make flush."

more business-minded than the others, set himself up as a self-appointed landlord and rented out rooms. The keeping room of the old house, with its hand-planed paneling, occasionally housed one of Douglas's two motorcycles, though their official accommodations were in the laundry room. The southeast corner room of the house would become Douglas's drafting room, where he transformed the plans of *Joe Lane* to become *Shenandoah*. (He would give Harvey Gamage the redrawn plans to work from in early 1963.) The room was also used for marine storage, bits of equipment Douglas had come across, old sails, ship models, rope, and other equipment.

The future captain of the *Shenandoah*—as described by Dan Goodenough, *Shenandoah*'s first cook—was exactly the sort of man who might have a laissez faire attitude toward the boarding house nature of his home. "Bob was a very sweet, shy, private person," remembered Goodenough, "and I felt very appreciated by him. John Mitchell, the galley boy, and I had all sorts of fun and games going on in *Shenandoah*'s galley. Sometimes we pretended to passengers that neither of us spoke a word of English. And Bob appreciated it and laughed at it, even though it was a bit disruptive at times. He seemed fine with it."

Rick Perras, who served two seasons on the schooner, roomed in Douglas's Vineyard Haven waterfront bunkhouse before each season began. He especially recalled Douglas's friend Chandler Moore, an astonishingly talented miniaturist who painted meticulously detailed pictures of wartime dogfights, square-rigged sailing vessels, and Liberty Ships attacked by German aircraft. Moore was genially and authentically retiring and eccentric. He dressed in khaki trousers and shirts and wore a pith helmet straight out of the era of British global imperialism. "I have never forgotten seeing Chandler Moore sleeping in his khaki uniform on Bob's couch and Bob's generosity, kindness, and protectiveness toward Chandler," he recalls. Perras was once asked to help Moore take one of his tiny ship models sailing on the Lagoon Pond in Vineyard Haven while Moore watched his vessel through a monocular and narrated the event for the two of them. "I have never seen anything like it. I also recall Bob personally taking me in the yawl boat from Tarpaulin Cove to Woods Hole to make it to a wedding"—a trip Douglas says today was a crazy decision that put the yawl boat at risk—"and my experience one week filling in as cook and deckhand on *Shenandoah* with a full complement of guests. I made a vodka-soaked watermelon fruit lunch that the guests liked. Bob didn't exactly endorse the departure from the menu. He may have frowned."

Douglas remembers that, later, his dad asked what to do with his West Chop house. "I said, 'I don't know. I've got a house here already.' So he sold the place, I think he told me, for $180,000. Christ, it's been on the market recently for $15 or $20 million, something like that. But they gutted the house, tore everything out of the inside—all the windows, doors, plaster, trim, everything—and made it more than twice as big as it was before, everything brand-new. At least six good houses on the west side of Vineyard Haven Harbor got bulldozed in this building craze that's going on. Makes you want to cry."

Chapter Four

The Downwind Leg Toward a Dream

ROBERT DOUGLAS IS AN UNPARALLELED accumulator of boats, big and little—wooden boats only, of course—boats that don't float but might one day, boats that will never float again, boats that hang from the ceiling in his office or under the porch roof outside the door. And pieces of boats—transoms, stems, knees of boats long since wrecked—and boat paintings, models, plans, photographs, quarterboards, anchors, capstans, and winches. His tugboat captain friend, the late Captain Roy Campbell, for whom, in 1970, Douglas built the 65-foot steel, twin-engine tugboat *Whitefoot*, sole asset of Whitefoot Towing and Salvage Company, once remarked to this writer, "Old son, if you split open that boy's head, you'd find a boat." Douglas would still have the captain's cap he earned at Camp Knowsley except that one day, sailing *Wideawake*, a saucy southwester blew it off his head and away.

Douglas's third boat—after the Menemsha and *Wideawake*—was his first schooner.

The boat suspended from the porch roof outside Douglas's office door suggests what awaits within.

She was *North Star,* a 28-foot double-ended Navy lifeboat that had previously been bought at auction by a handy fellow who had decked her over and built a cockpit and simple accommodations below: two bunks and a shelf to serve as a galley. Douglas, anticipating his freshman summer vacation from Northwestern and wanting a boat to cruise in, found *North Star* while visiting his friend Roy Goff in Philadelphia and nosing around local boatyards. "I went looking for a boat, and we found *North Star*. Dad said, 'Keep it reasonable,' and I did," he remembers. "Later, Roy and I sailed her up to the Vineyard."

In the winter of 1955–56, he sailed *North Star* down the Inland Waterway. He sold her in January 1956 as his Air Force commitment began, but not before she led him to a connection with Havilah 'Buds' Hawkins, who would nurture and guide the course of Douglas's still unfocused enthusiasm for sailing and Martha's Vineyard. Like the example his father set for him, like the mother who kissed him goodnight, like Curtis Cate who took Douglas under his wing at the Cate School, like Frank Agnew, his flying instructor in the Air Force and lifelong friend and sailing companion, Hawkins became a mentor, inspiring and guiding Douglas as he slowly settled on a course no one had imagined for him.

Aboard *North Star* on her Vineyard Haven mooring one summer afternoon, not sailing but repairing and improving his new command, Douglas noticed a Friendship sloop entering the harbor under sail, obviously intending to anchor and spend the night. Friendship sloops are distinctive workboat types, originally used for near-shore fishing, with big cockpits for handling the catch and small cabins to shelter the crew when necessary. The name came from the town of Friendship, Maine, where they were much prized and widely used. Picturesque and considered handy and good sailers, the gaff-rigged sloops were often adapted and later built specifically for use as pleasure craft.

Inside Douglas's office.

The Friendship sloop Douglas saw was towing a light, lovely, double-ended rowing boat known as a peapod, likewise common on the Maine coast for fishing and waterfront work. Peapods, built of cedar and oak, possess a striking sheer and a deserved reputation for easy rowing and towing; some had sailing rigs. Douglas's eye was immediately drawn to it. Upon introducing himself to Jerry Smith, owner of the sloop, and asking where he could get a peapod like that, he learned that Havilah Hawkins of Sedgwick, Maine, built them for sale at $150 apiece.

In the spring of 1953, his sophomore year at Northwestern, Douglas drove his 1929 Model A Ford with the mail-truck body from Chicago to Sedgwick to collect the peapod he had paid Hawkins to build for him over the winter. Hawkins was not at home, but Mary Day, the builder's wife, was. Douglas loaded the peapod on the roof of his Model A and started for the Vineyard. He hadn't gone far when he encountered Hawkins in his pickup truck where Route 15 crests Caterpillar Hill in Sedgwick. Hawkins recognized his handiwork perched atop the oncoming vehicle and flagged Douglas down.

A video documentary from offcenterharbor.com describes Hawkins this way: "Sometime in the late 1940s stepped Havilah 'Budsy' Hawkins. The son of an artist, and something of an artist himself, Budsy was either a man behind or ahead of his times, depending on how you looked at it." (Hawkins was known as Bud, Budsy, or Buds. Douglas always called him Buds.) Boatbuilder, schooner captain, artist, and business-man, Hawkins discerned in Douglas a like-minded young soul with a gifted eye for the grace of old-fashioned wooden boats, especially cleverly crafted, easy-sailing schooners with historic pedigrees. They talked and kept in touch while Douglas finished North-western and began his Air Force service.

Hawkins owned and operated two old schooners in the passenger trade out of Cam-den, the *Stephen Taber* and the *Alice Wentworth*. The *Taber* was a veteran of the coastwise freight trade up and down the Maine coast, in and out of rivers and island harbors where loads of ice, lumber, cordwood, granite, and other goods were regular cargoes. The *Went-worth* had been built in Connecticut in 1863 as the *Lizzie A. Tolles*. The *Tolles* started in the freight business but was not based in Maine until she was bought by the Stevens brothers of Wells, Maine, and renamed in 1905. Later, a widely known, eccentric, and admired seaman named Zebulon Tilton of Martha's Vineyard bought her, and the ancient schoo-ner became a familiar sight in Vineyard waters and elsewhere around southern New England between 1921 and 1943.

Hawkins, a New Jersey native, had studied art at Boston Museum School, at the Art Students League of New York, and at the National Academy of Art (also in New York). He had also studied yacht design at the Massachusetts Institute of Technology. In his Sedgwick barn beside the Benjamin River was a ship model he had crafted and the lines he had taken off it for a brand-new schooner he wanted to build. She would be the *Mary Day*, named after Hawkins's wife. Built at Harvey Gamage's South Bristol shipyard just before the *Shenandoah*, the *Mary Day* was to become the first Maine schooner purpose-built for the passenger trade. Hawkins and his family would sail her for thirty-five years.

During and after his Air Force hitch, Douglas spent time at the family home in Lake Forest when he wasn't on active duty or on the Vineyard. James and Elinor Douglas were in Washington most of the time, and the big family house was mostly empty and lonely, so Douglas moved into the barn apartment with his father's gardener and caretaker, Hubert Klaren, who had held that position since Douglas's father had bought the house. "He was a wonderful old guy I had known since I was a kid, and he was very clever at fixing things, and in the barn below the apartment there was plenty of room where we had Model A Fords apart," Douglas recalls. There, Douglas rehabbed the Model A in which he traveled the East Coast, visiting friends and buying or trading skiffs and small sailboats.

Just before joining the Air Force, in the winter of 1955, Douglas bought a Bahama sailing dinghy which he used in Panama City while stationed at Graham Air Force Base. Douglas admired the lovely, handy craft. Later he loaded the dinghy on the Model A and drove it to the Vineyard, where he stored it at his father's house..

One trip Douglas made during the month's convalescent leave granted him in early 1957 by the Air Force after the crash that damaged his back took him to Wiscasset, Maine, where he visited Alex and Sally Brown, friends he had made on a boat in Miami while in the Air Force. "And it just happened to be—I don't know if I planned it— a weekend, and I bummed a ride on one of Buds Hawkins's schooners, the *Stephen Taber*. I remember we got off in Stonington, and I had a terrible time getting home, because I had left my 1956 GMC Carryall in a parking lot at the Camden shipyard on the other side of Penobscot Bay. This would have been my first look at the windjammer business."

The experience did not trigger dreams of a windjammer of his own. Douglas bought his first sizable, live-aboard boat, the 48-foot teak ketch *Ayuthia,* a month or two before leaving the Air Force in 1958. "I got paid $3,000 a year in the Air Force, and I put that money in the bank. I was going to isolate that to build a boat, and I just about did. I paid $12,000 for *Ayuthia*."

He had *Ayuthia* delivered from Maryland to Vineyard Haven, where he discovered that the surveyor he'd hired to evaluate the keel-centerboard ketch had omitted a problem or two from his report. "He lied to me," is how Douglas puts it. The biggest problem was with the steel centerboard and its steel trunk, both of which had rusted so extensively that the board could not be lowered. Douglas replaced the centerboard with one that was operable but chose to postpone repairs to the trunk. He replaced the shaft of

Douglas found the teak ketch *Ayuthia* in the summer of 1958 in Galesville, Maryland. He bought her from Jan Miles, and she was his first sizable cruising boat. He had saved all his Air Force pay, which amounted to just what he needed to buy her. He soon repainted her white.

the steering wheel with a longer one and installed a wheel of a smaller diameter, making it possible for him to sit at the back of the cockpit to steer. He also replaced the ketch's engine. He did the work himself, and then he went cruising in *Ayuthia*, the largest vessel he had yet commanded.

"By the time I got out of the Air Force," Douglas recalls, "I wondered what the hell was I going to do. I thought, 'Well, I'm not going to plan too far ahead. For five years I'm going to fuck off, not going to put any hooks down, or at least not put down two anchors.' And it worked out. . . .

"I spent the winters of 1958 – 59 and 1959 – 60 going south and back in the Inland Waterway, motoring in the Ditch," as the Intracoastal Waterway between the Chesapeake Bay and Florida is known. He cruised in the Bahamas with his brother John, and he spent Thanksgiving with his stepmother and father in their Georgetown house and Christmas with his whole family in a house his parents had rented at Hog Island in the

Bahamas, now known as Paradise Island. In the spring of 1959 and again in 1960 he sailed *Ayuthia* to Maine, leaving her on one of Hawkins's moorings in Camden's inner harbor while he worked with Hawkins on the *Stephen Taber* from April to September. He towed the Bahama sailing dinghy to Maine in the spring of 1960. That dinghy eventually graduated to hanging in davits aboard *Shenandoah* as the captain's gig.

One spring afternoon in 1960, sitting in the Hawkins' living room in Sedgwick with the Benjamin River estuary sparkling outside the window, Douglas's eyes fell on

Douglas reaching along the west side of the Exhumas in *Ayuthia* with his brother John. Built in Thailand in 1936, *Ayuthia* was drawn by the English designer Maurice Griffiths. Bob lived aboard her on a mooring in Camden's inner harbor while working for Hawkins aboard the *Stephen Taber* and the *Alice Wentworth*.

Howard I. Chapelle's *History of American Sailing Ships.* Chapelle was a marine historian, a naval architect, and curator of the Watercraft Collection at the Smithsonian Institution. Anyone who cared about maritime heritage knew Chapelle's work. Leafing through the book, Douglas came upon the original plans for the *Joseph Lane*, reproduced by Chapelle to illustrate the story of her design and construction in 1848 – 49. She was one of a new class of fast topsail schooners designed in 1848, larger than any vessels built previously for the Revenue Marine (later renamed the Revenue Cutter Service, forerunner of the US Coast Guard). "The lack of interest among American marine historians in the United States Revenue Marine is difficult to explain, for the service has had a remarkable career, full of incidents of historical importance, and was founded some years before the Navy," Chapelle wrote:

> During the sailing ship period the Revenue Marine was engaged in other work than mere enforcement of revenue laws, for its duties included suppression of the slave trade and piracy, life-saving and salvage work at sea, carrying of government dispatches and diplomats and assisting the Navy in wartime, all with their many incidental adventures. . . . No Revenue service abroad has had a more interesting history than the American corps. . . .
>
> Alexander Hamilton, first Secretary of the Treasury, received his portfolio from Washington at the age of 32, soon after the latter's inauguration in 1789. Hamilton understood the necessity of employing watercraft in the collection of revenue duties and in the enforcement of revenue laws. The Congress authorized the new Revenue Marine in March of 1790, and Congress appropriated funds for the construction of revenue cutters in April.
>
> In 1848, it was decided that new cutters were needed and seven were ordered, at least four of them being sister-ships. . . . The plans of the new cutters called for very fast fore topsail schooners on the most advanced clipper model of the time. . . . The *Campbell* was built at Portsmouth, Virginia during 1848 – 49 by Graves and Fenbie. In 1851 she was badly damaged when she was run down by a schooner during a gale and required extensive repairs. In 1855 she was renamed the *Joseph Lane* (referred to officially and in service as the *Joe Lane*). She ended her career on the Pacific Coast, where she was sold in 1869.

Her plans . . . are the only ones available for her class. . . . She was a long, low, keel schooner of about 102 feet on deck, 100 feet 4 inches on the load waterline, 23 feet extreme beam, and 9 feet 7½ inches draft. The *Lane* represents, in a general way, the cutters built afterwards; the round stern, low freeboard and the beautiful clipper bow surmounted by an eagle with outspread wings. . . .

Here was a design—bigger than a coasting schooner, rakish-looking, fast-sailing, lissome, complicated, sleek, and beautiful—that spoke to the 28-year-old Douglas. When he left Hawkins's house that day, he took a vision of *Joe Lane* with him.

During that summer of 1960, Douglas first met Charlene Lapointe of Padanarum, a village in South Dartmouth, Massachusetts, when the *Taber* anchored for the night in Bucks Harbor. Charlene was working aboard the three-masted windjammer *Victory Chimes*, also anchored in Bucks. Ten years later, Robert and Charlene would marry, but there was no hint of that future in their first cameo meeting.

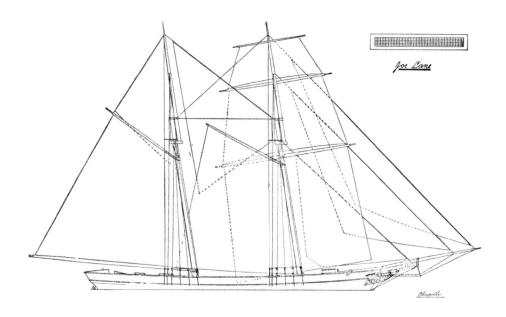

The rakish-looking *Joe Lane* as Douglas discovered her in Howard I. Chapelle's *History of American Sailing Ships*. "The plans of the new cutters called for very fast fore topsail schooners on the most advanced clipper model of the time," Chapelle wrote.

But time began to compress and accelerate for Douglas in other ways that summer, propelling him toward the decision that would anchor the rest of his life. There is no evidence of a conscious plan, and he is convinced that he was utterly innocent of any faintly twinkling subconscious plan to do what he would shortly do. He did not know what was coming and was not aware of being on the lookout for it.

"A family who booked a week on the *Taber* while I was mate had just been down to Nova Scotia and had stopped off in Lunenburg. They came back with pictures and a story about the *Bounty*," whose construction was nearing completion at Smith & Rhuland Shipyard in Lunenburg. The HMS *Bounty* replica was being built for Metro-Goldwyn-Mayer (MGM Studios) to be the central prop in its 1962 film *Mutiny on the Bounty*.

In company with Buds and Mary Day Hawkins, Douglas flew to Lunenburg to ask about a job and was told he could have a crewman's berth if he wanted it. Hawkins urged him to sign on—indeed, Hawkins himself would have made the trip except that his business and family responsibilities, including two young children, made it impossible—but still Douglas wavered. "I said, 'Can I sleep on it?' They hadn't hired a captain, and that worried me. So I remember I didn't sleep for a good day and night, but in the end I signed up.

"I stayed three weeks, I guess, in Lunenburg before she sailed. What a wonderful, friendly town. Wonderful, wonderful people. And then I was on the boat for three months or so for the voyage to Tahiti. Nobody wanted to go sailing. It wasn't a sailboat, it was just a movie prop, it really was. But still, I had a chance to get aloft and stow sail and play the whole thing out. She was only 118 feet long. She really wasn't that big a boat."

Chapter Five

Tahiti Bound

METRO-GOLDEN-MAYER's ship-rigged *Bounty*, Captain Ellsworth Trask Coggins, departed Lunenburg, Nova Scotia, on October 26, 1960, bound through the Panama Canal for Tahiti, a voyage of about 7,000 sea miles. Twenty-eight-year-old deckhand Robert Douglas recorded the occasion in the first entry of the log he kept daily. Young as he was, and despite his modest sailing experience—limited to small daysailers, a few months as mate aboard Maine schooners, a few trips down and back up the East Coast's Intracoastal Waterway and to the Bahamas in a converted lifeboat and a 48-foot ketch—Douglas nevertheless kept a detailed, formal log as a seasoned mariner might have done. He was conscious of how he inscribed his observations. He had bought an enormous, hard-bound Minute Book, eight by fourteen-and-a-half inches, in which to record not only the daily incidents of the journey but his impressions as well. Perhaps he imagined himself a ship's officer one day, even a captain, whose record was official and likely to be preserved for historians to pore over.

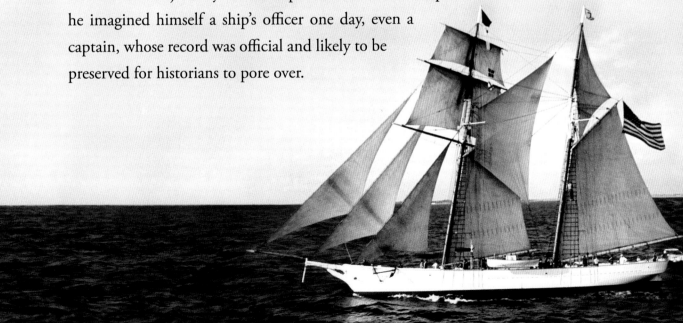

Each day's remarks opened with "The day commences . . ." and closed with "So ends this day," a decidedly oceangoing construct. Of HMS *Bounty*'s leave-taking from her builder's dock, he wrote:

Day commences cold, overcast, fresh NW breeze. Cast off dock lines and backed out of the government wharf at 8:30 am. Once with the engines ahead three long blasts . . . were given on the *Bounty*'s horn, and several vessels responded. . . . We headed out south of Cross Island. Out past the Ovens the sea had begun to get a good lump on it. The fore topsail was set and the fore topmast staysail, and with this sail we carried on till 5 pm with engines too. A good lump of sea was on all day, with the figurehead getting half a dunking most of the time, only occasional spray on deck.

At 12 am, the watches were called. I got the 4-8, the first mate's watch. . . . Clewed up the fore topsail at 5 pm and set the main topmast staysail and mizzen topmast staysail. Then with the other two watches, which had been called, went aloft and stowed the fore topsail, and it was a good job holding on. . . . Went below at 8 pm . . . and what a stink in the galley, devastating combination of backed-up sink and beef curry. The cook certainly has

HMS *Bounty II*, which Douglas shipped aboard in late 1960, is shown here under not-quite-full sail (mizzen topsail and topgallant not set) on Lake Michigan near the Port of Chicago, participating in the 2010 Great Lake Tall Ship Challenge. *(Photo by Dan Kasberger)*

an iron gut. 10 pm, the wind still west, fine lump on, low clouds, no stars, and cold. So ends this day.

Captain Coggins, 1914 – 1987, had had a long and varied career. Fishing at night as a youngster while attending a two-room school in the day, he leapt at the chance, in his teens, for a berth on a Nova Scotian schooner carrying cargoes to the West Indies. He was ambitious and competent, particularly at navigation, of which he became an instructor to Canadian Navy inductees in World War II. In 1960, MGM Studios hired him away from the Smith & Rhuland Shipyard, where he was employed running small craft around the yard, to be master of HMS *Bounty* for the duration of her brief movie career. Later, Coggins would be named captain of the big fishing schooner replica *Bluenose II*, a fore-and-aft schooner of 130 feet. She too was built at Smith & Rhuland, launched in July 1963. Coggins also had experience running a small ketch, donated to the Canadian Navy as a training vessel, on a voyage to the Canadian west coast, but he had had no previous experience with square-rigged vessels. Douglas was the only American in the *Bounty* crew. The mate was Ross MacKay. The bosun was George Snow, the only sailor in the *Bounty* crew with square-rig experience, having served aboard the three-masted barkentine *Sunbeam*.

Douglas admits to being seasick on the Tahiti passage, but he qualifies that, saying that the distress occurred only after leaving the dock at Lunenburg and again leaving the Canal Zone. Once well at sea, the symptoms abated. He recalled that Roy Campbell, his Vineyard friend and the captain of the 65-foot tugboat *Whitefoot* that Douglas would build in 1970, once amused himself by presenting Douglas with a birthday gift of a single roller skate. Campbell explained that one skate was all Douglas needed, because when sailing he liked to keep one foot on shore.

With both feet well offshore, late in the afternoon of "28 Oct 60" (Douglas used a version of the military format for expressing dates throughout his log), two days out from Lunenburg, *Bounty* found herself in squally weather.

Our watch began at 4 pm and shortly called all hands to snug the after shrouds on main and fore. Spanker and main staysail had been taken down during the afternoon. By 6:30 pm it was blowing 50 mph for sure, accompanied with driving rain and wind, and wind and rain kept up till 7:30 pm, when the sky came clear and the breeze began to moderate. The wind had shifted to E, and by 9 pm sea is considerably smoother. Beautiful night and was so in a wild way during the blow, for the moon was showing through the ragged low bank of fast-moving clouds and its silver on the gray waves was a fine sight. But the rigging outlined against the scudding clouds and the half moon vied for honors. By 9:45 pm the fo'c'sle is much more liveable, and it is time to turn in. So ends this day.

Sixty miles northwest of Bermuda, "it seems the air conditioning outfit is out of whack. The fo'c'sle can fairly well do without it, but the engine room is over 120 degrees, and the after accommodations are very warm. 9:00 pm, cool beautiful evening, a bit warm in the fo'c'sle. So ends this day."

The weather, the food, the beauty of sea and sky, and the irregular habits of the air conditioning were persistent topics in Douglas's log, but as *Bounty* ranged farther from the yard where she was built and rigged, what increasingly caught Douglas's eye were the details of her complicated rig that had not been worked out before sailing. A portion of the entry for October 31 describes the chaos:

> Day commences overcast intermittent rain, wind W, course still 190 degrees. Miserably hot night, vessel rolling like mad. Spent the forenoon under fore topmast staysail and mizzen topmast staysail. During the early part of the afternoon we shook out the fore course and full reefed the fore topsail and set it. Mass confusion reigns. No one in command has the slightest idea what to do except George Snow, so he is sent aloft. What a screwy vessel. Spent the evening watch coiling down and rearranging things around the main fife rail. Took my trick at the wheel, 200 degrees the course. . . .

The *Bounty* transited the Mona Passage between Hispaniola and Puerto Rico, crossed the Caribbean, and approached Cristobal in the Canal Zone. Some cloddish details of *Bounty*'s rig, which had not really been completed before the departure from Lunenburg, had proved a trial for officers and crew through the first leg of the voyage. Jim Havens, MGM's second unit director and the overseer of *Bounty*'s construction, was aboard for the trip and contributed to some of the hubbubs.

7 Nov 60: Day commences warm, overcast, light NE breeze. Vessel still under fore topmast staysail, fore topsail, main topsail. We set the mizzen topsail around 7:00 am, and do you know who threw another tantrum when certain buntlines had the slack taken out of them? Strange talk of imaginary squalls was bruited about in the 4-to-8 watch. Around 11:00 am, the place went nuts with Havens screaming all hands. A bit of a rain squall had taken the vessel aback and a few yards needed bracing around. He doesn't know the difference between topsail and topgallant, let alone where their braces belay. But soon all was cleared and we proceeded under full steam. Passed through the jetties around 5:30 pm and soon had pilots and what all aboard. A competent pilot, I must say, and as smooth a job of docking as one is liable to see anywhere. And at about 6:30 pm we were securely tied to the end of Pier #10 Cristobal C.Z. Customs and immigration were soon aboard. Mail also, best of all. And soon the troops were ashore for an evening of debauchery, and I took several beers at the Club Florida. Fine floor show, a cruise around town, and back aboard. Fine, cool, clear night. The vessel is quiet and cooling off. The engine rooms must be down to 100 degrees for now, ha ha. So ends this day.

The problem with the buntlines, which had been measured and installed by the rigging crew before leaving Lunenburg, was a particular disappointment to Douglas. It represented the sort of issues common in a rig installed by inexperienced sailors. The buntlines control the center of a square sail, securing the bunt against the yard it sets from when it is furled. To set the sail, the buntlines are slacked and overhauled by the sailors aloft so that the canvas can drop from the yard without resistance. When the sail is to be taken in, the buntlines are drawn up. The clew lines are similar but control the sail's bottom corners, or clews. In measuring clew lines and buntlines, the rigger must calculate liberally for the run up to the sail, through its cringles or grommets—or, on a very large sail, through blocks—and back down to the deck, so that the lines run easily when overhauled and leave plenty of length on deck for belaying and coiling. Douglas and his crewmates discovered that on *Bounty,* when the square sails were set, the bitter ends of the buntlines and clewlines, all too short, waved in the breeze above the deck.

Douglas was not yet a hands-on veteran or even a practiced neophyte in the management of a vessel with square sails, but his log makes clear that it was a subject that

In the seafaring tradition, 28-year-old Bob Douglas recorded a daily log of his voyage to Tahiti.

captured his attention. The ship-rigged *Bounty* could set two jibs, four square sails on the foremast, four on the mainmast, and three on the mizzen above the fore-and-aft spanker. The entries in his daily log reveal a consuming attention to the rig: to the joy of being aloft in it and to the need for keeping a sharp eye out for how it ought to work and how to solve the problems. More than the weather, more than the food, more than his fellow crewmen or the air conditioning, his entries reflect his persistent self-education in the ways of a square-rigged vessel. Unasked, working in his fo'c's'le bunk, Douglas made a diagram showing where each of the lines—buntlines, clewlines, leech lines, halyards, sheets, braces—for each of the sails and yards should belay after each was used. He thumbtacked his handiwork to the bulkhead next to the ladder leading to the deck. The next day the mate saw it and took it with him to the deck.

Bounty and *Shenandoah* were somewhat similar in size. *Bounty* was 90 feet 10 inches on deck compared with *Shenandoah,* 108; and *Bounty's* maximum beam was 30 feet and her depth 14, versus *Shenandoah's* 27-foot width and 11-foot depth. But the outstanding difference between the two was their shapes. The real *Bounty* was a collier (originally called *Berthia)* of about 90 feet. Bought by the British in 1787, she was renamed and remade to carry a cargo of breadfruit from Tahiti for transplanting in the West Indies, an experiment designed to find a crop that would flourish in the West Indian climate and soils and help the British feed their plantation slaves. The Royal Navy added armaments and detailed a crew of 46 to sail her. She was selected because she was capacious enough to accommodate the crew, necessary armaments, ammunition, and the plants. What there was no room for—critically, as it turned out—was a detachment of Royal Marines to help Captain William Bligh keep order should the need arise.

On the foredeck during the voyage, Douglas liked to watch as *Bounty's* bluff, rounded bow shouldered its way into the seas, pushing up a great bow wave as if it were an enormous soup ladle forcing its way, business-end foremost, through the ocean. Later he would occasionally perch in the chains below *Shenandoah's* bowsprit to watch as her bow sliced through the sea, in sharp contrast with the *Bounty's*. *Bounty* carried her width forward and aft along nearly her entire length. Years later, Douglas used his two index fingers to trace two transverse ship sections in the air: first, the graceful shape of a wine glass, and then the voluminous section of a barge or *Berthia* the collier. His eye finds satisfaction in the former.

The ship forged into the Pacific after transiting the canal, with the crew, including Douglas, sick. In light southwesterlies and frequent deluges, her twin Caterpillar diesels rumbling below, *Bounty* set mostly jibs, staysails, and spanker. A common practice among careful masters of square-rigged ships was to reduce sail during the evening watch, particularly the square sails; this was particularly advised aboard *Bounty*, whose haphazard arrangement of sheets, halyards, and braces, often not belayed to the same pin twice, could compromise the vessel and its crew in a sudden, nasty midwatch squall.

On November 16, Douglas noted, "5 weeks ago today I started to work for this crazy outfit." The next day, leaving the Galapagos below the horizon a hundred miles to port, he recorded the loss of one of the two stowaways that had taken up residence on *Bounty*: "poor old hawk glided off into the drink at 5:30 am. I guess he preferred a quick death to slow torture aboard." Douglas had learned what he wanted to learn and discovered himself ready to move on.

Bounty crossed the International Dateline on the evening of November 20, but the traditional and much-anticipated celebration had to be postponed to the following day because sail changes occupied the crew. According to Douglas's November 21 entry:

> His highness Neptune came aboard, and all us polliwogs got shampooed and etc. and duly became shellbacks. Ross MacKay was a fine Neptune. Newcombe, Hughie, and Ivan were Davey Jones and two goon girls respectively, and cook was the barber. All in all it was a fine afternoon. An hour on our watch there was a fine dinner of corn, pork chops and potatoes. And fresh bread. Took in the topgallants, furled the fore topgallant and had just clewed up the main topgallant when a blast of black smoke issued out of the main hatch followed by Keith [the third engineer] and the call of 'FIRE.'
>
> The engines' exhausts went black and both engines went out—or just one, reports are mixed. We soon had both auxiliary engines running, fire pump and standby generator. . . . With much doing and chasing around, things came under control. A fine supply of food and blankets were on the fo'c'sle head, and considerable progress had been made in getting the covers off the two boats. By 7:30 pm it looked like we could straighten things out.

They did "straighten things out," and happily there was no need for the food and blankets or for the lifeboats. Several vessels responded to the "standby SOS" *Bounty* sent out, the closest just 70 miles away. This was the second time the Caterpillar engines with their red-hot exhausts had threatened to set *Bounty* ablaze. Neither exhaust had been equipped with a cooling water jacket.

> *8:30 pm*: Both engines are at cruising RPMs again and below things are settling down. 9:30, fine, clear night, south wind, course 230 degrees. And we will hope a third time doesn't finish us off, for we've still got 2,000 miles to go.

The next day brought another fire, this time the wiring and the rubber hoses connected to the generator, all proximate to the hot engine exhausts, but the blaze was quickly extinguished.

There were splendid days, of course, and Douglas grants them their due.

25 Nov 60: Spent most of the morning sacked in. Finished up the Bounty Trilogy in the PM. When the 4-to-8 came, on deck at 4. What a sight to behold. All the royals were set. The afterguard is really getting bold. A beautiful day. Fresh southeast breeze, the sea a fabulous blue, and the old sled is really slipping along, a bit over 10. I guess that's about the best she can do, for she does push a fine pile of water ahead of her. Spliced a few fathoms to the port main clewline grommet. A fine dinner of cold potato salad, tuna, shrimp, and blueberry pie. Clewed up the royals after dinner and furled them. Things are looking up on the old vessel, for this is the first night the crowd aft has had the bravery to set anything above the topsails at night. And we are making good time. At this rate we are expected to sail into Tahiti a week from tomorrow night. So ends this Day.

27 Nov 60: On deck at 10:00 am for a game of wearing ship. All kinds of screeching and ridiculous orders.

4 Dec 60: A fine sight was in view to the southeast. Tahiti, her jagged outline clear against the starlit sky, and Moorea to the SW. Venus Point flashing to the south. Steamed slowly back and forth 6 miles or so off all night, when we headed for Venus Point, picked up the pilot and customs officials and then with all square sails but the royals set and the jib and fore topmast staysail, we steamed in around Dolphin Bank and dropped anchor Matavai Bay.

Soon had all sails clewed up, and a fine big brand-new double-hulled canoe put off from the beach with band and officials. . . . Soon got the hook and steamed out and down to Papeete. Seems to have caused a bit of a stir, as about the whole population of the island seemed to be onboard.

The moviemaking began immediately. Early-morning Papeete was quiet on December 5, 1960, when *Bounty*'s crew was roused to begin offloading gear that would not be needed during the filming. The crew threw open the hatches to gather the sailing equipment that would not be useful to the filmmakers and would be sent ashore, including *Bounty*'s longboat, which would live for the duration of filming on the Papeete dock. Tahitian workers hired by MGM crowded aboard to clear the decks. Douglas spent most of the day in the rigging, cutting off projecting bolts, re-leading halyards, and re-lashing ratlines and battens. During a trip to a hardware store in Papeete, he saw William A. Robinson, the sailor and author of *Ten Thousand Leagues Over the Sea* (1932). Robinson had made the voyage to Tahiti in his 32-foot Alden ketch *Svaap*. "I'd like to have a chat with him one of these days," Douglas wrote in his journal. At the MGM Studios quarters, Douglas was fitted for the costume he would wear while playing the sailor Ellison, one of the three who get hanged in the film.

Impatient with the disorderly work belowdecks by the *Bounty* crew abetted by the throng of Tahitian workers, Douglas found more to do aloft. For example, he sawed off and rounded the sharp corners of the main topmast crosstrees and trestle trees to make it less likely the sail would be damaged from chafe when the yards were braced up sharp. By Christmas Eve, his disappointment had risen to out-and-out contempt for the enterprise he had been attached to for the past three months. Certainly his views were colored by the imminence of the warm family holiday he would miss. Half a world away from home, he was lonely and eager to end this journey.

> *24 Dec 60*: I had the watch till 8:00 pm, then took a spin downtown on the Vespa to a busy spot. Got good and wet on the way out and back about 10:30 pm and sacked in. Still more light rain.
>
> I'm afraid I can think of several better places to spend Christmas Eve and with some people I love, but this neck of the woods is my doing, and if I had half a brain I would have flown out of here last Thursday and would now be in Washington, DC. But if I have any measure of mind or sense of the value of time, next week this time I will be there, and with the *Bounty* far behind me.
>
> Not even one sign of Christmas aboard her, other than a few Christmas cards, not a pine tree at any masthead. Well, tomorrow, if I've got any

sense, I'll start the wheels rolling and get off this poor old unfortunate vessel, the boat that really could have been something. Enough.

Christmas day dawned with a "drunken and drinking hoard" in the fo'c's'le. Douglas finished or nearly finished letters to Frank Agnew, his friend and flight instructor, and to Adrian Lane, captain at the time of the Woods Hole Oceanographic Institution's research vessel *Atlantis*, a double-ended steel ketch. And he recalled other, happier Christmases with brothers, parents, and friends.

On January 19, 1961, Douglas left Papeete for Los Angeles on a ticket costing 37,640 French francs.

Chapter Six

Joe Lane, the Clincher

WHILE DOUGLAS HAD BEEN on his way to Tahiti, Buds Hawkins had sold both of his schooners in the course of one lucky, frantic week. "Two people wandered in from the street," Douglas remembers. "One bought the *Taber,* and the other was a crazy lady who preferred to be called Commodore White. She had been on the *Taber* for a week in the summer when I worked as mate, and she bought Hawkins's long-lived coasting freighter *Alice Wentworth*—which, by the way, had sailed out of the Vineyard for a couple of decades under Captain Zebulon Tilton. So, Buds sold both boats within a week. It was just one of those crazy things."

A fire had burned the handsome barn where Hawkins built his peapods, consuming the model he had made of the *Mary Day*, but he still had the plans and offsets for his future schooner, and she existed with perfect clarity in his mind's eye.

She was to be a brand-new passenger schooner that would suit his business plan perfectly, reduce the maintenance and repair budget, and operate as economically as possible.

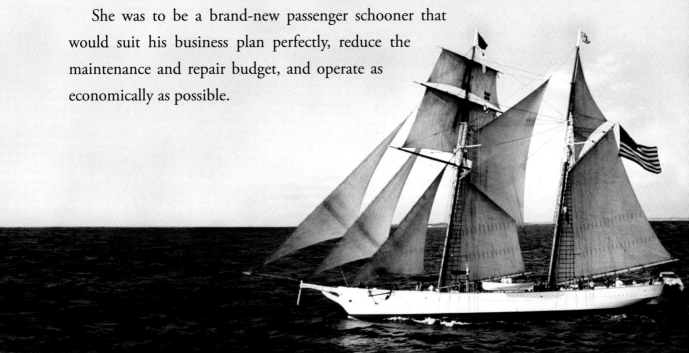

It took little time to make a new model, and then Hawkins "began to wander around, looking for a builder for his new boat," Douglas remembers. He found Harvey Gamage.

During World War II, Harvey Gamage's business had prospered building mine-sweepers for the Navy. After the war, the yard's bread and butter became lobster boats, yachts, and a great many offshore draggers and scallopers fishing out of East Coast ports such as New Bedford, Massachusetts. "Harvey had one dragger building on spec that was still unlaunched and unsold," Douglas says. "There was an empty space on the eastern ways next to it. The dragger was all painted, and Buds said, 'Harvey, build me a schooner.' Harvey agreed, and the price was $37,500 for the 88-foot *Mary Day* as a bare hull, all caulked and painted but no interior, no rig on the boat. So off they went, and soon the keel was laid."

Mary Day sports two gaff topsails in this recent photograph. She was launched without them, but Havilah Hawkins built her masts with the ironwork in place to add topmasts when and if they were ever wanted, and that moment arrived in the 1970s. "I guess we were bored," said Havilah's son Ronnie, who fashioned the spars. It was around that time that *Mary Day* had a part in the filming of the 1977 television film *Captains Courageous*, and fore and main gaff topsails were attractive enhancements. Douglas is convinced that *Shenandoah*'s tall rig, with square sails and topmasts, inspired the Maine schooner fleet to follow his lead. Rebuilt in 1999 – 2000, *Mary Day* is now owned and operated by Barry and Jen King.
(*Blaine Harrington photo courtesy Alamy Stock Photo*)

Back in Maine to visit Hawkins at Gamage's yard, Douglas found himself drawn into the *Mary Day* construction. "And I was betwixt and between after getting back from Tahiti," Douglas remembers. "So, Buds put me up near Harvey's at the Coveside Inn in Christmas Cove, and I worked as his gofer."

The coastwise sailing freighters that were common as mud up and down the East Coast in the late nineteenth and early twentieth centuries found fewer and fewer cargoes by the 1930s. Enterprising Maine mariners could buy the healthiest of the surviving schooners at modest prices, sometimes no more than $1,000, convert them to carry passengers on summer cruises, do the maintenance and repair work themselves, and find themselves in business—a popular and growing business at that. When an elderly repurposed schooner needed more repair or reconstruction than was economical, the owner might run it onto a near-shore ledge off an unoccupied island and burn it. There was certain to be a replacement available, modestly priced, a bit younger perhaps, in need of less reconstruction and with the promise of a few useful years left in her.

Douglas's deepening attachment to the Maine windjammer owners, their vessels, and their trade developed in him a sympathetic understanding of the place they had made for themselves in the extension of what had come to be known as America's Golden Age of Sail. "When traditions get interrupted, a whole lifestyle, its techniques, its knowhow, all those things are lost," Douglas says. "If it hadn't been for one guy, Frank Swift, the schooner-freighter trail might have ended. In the late 1930s, Swift was mixed up in the entertainment business in New York City. He had summers off, and he saw the chance of getting into what has been referred to as the windjammer trade. And at that time, you had a significant coasting fleet of small schooners owned and operating in the Penobscot Bay area. One or two were built down in Maine, but I think most of them had been built in Connecticut and the western end of Long Island Sound, where builders had access to white oak, something absent from the forests Down East. For instance, Hawkins's *Stephen Taber* was built in Glenwood Landing, Long Island, and the *Alice Wentworth* was built as a freighter in Norwalk, Connecticut.

"The reason those boats moved to Maine when they did was because trucking took over freight delivery to the west, but you still had islands and no bridges in Maine. So you had a fleet of boats that showed up because they were available. They no longer had a business to the west. There was still a lot of kiln wood being cut on Maine's offshore islands that needed to be lugged around. A lot of the schooners were used for carrying the firewood, and they were built for carrying cargoes of bricks, too. They wound up in Maine because there was still a job for them there.

"You've always got to have a spark plug, and Frank Swift was it. When cargo carrying dried up even in Maine, requiring the changeover to what was referred to as 'walking freight' loads, Swift was there. It wasn't impossible to end up with a perfectly usable schooner for under a thousand dollars. At one point he owned five of them at the same time. And there were lots of retired old guys around that didn't have anything to do, so there was no problem getting an experienced crew together, and there was no Coast

Guard inspection or licensing in anything under 700 tons, so you didn't even have to call the Coast Guard. You didn't have to have a licensed crewmember or captain. It was very simple then to get into the windjammer business. And it thrived, relatively speaking, whatever 'thrived' means. If that continuum hadn't been set up and Frank Swift hadn't showed up at that time, you'd have lost a tradition.

"It's a really unusual trade. Even now, the owners are the skippers. There's no other business that works like that. Most 707 pilots don't own their planes. But the technology is fairly simple. Hawkins used to ground his schooners on the beach. He built himself a dry dock in a depression just to the north of his father's boatyard in Sedgwick and built doors that floated in place, and he'd put the schooner in, tie the masthead off to posts on the side, and put the doors in the way and let the tide run out. And he had his own boatyard. So it was a technology that was possible. He could replace the deck and build new spars. That kind of involvement, which is unusual, kept up in the windjammer business. The change of the schooner business kept the tradition going just long enough for the new money to commit. It was not a matter of capitalization back in those days. You could get in for almost nothing. Now new boats cost about $3 million.

"So, I occasionally think of what a debt was owed by the early operators to Frank Swift. And he hung around the Maine coast just long enough. The coastal Mainiacs who lived there held the windjammers in complete disregard, even calling them 'skin boats.' I never could figure why. The schooner operators were making real dollars. They could live off that income.

"So, this continuum is there for Buds, and Harvey had one dragger he had built on spec and finished, and it was unsold in his shed. That was the perfect time to walk in there and say, 'Harvey, I'd like to build a schooner,' which is what Hawkins did."

Douglas's three-month adventure aboard *Bounty* had disappointed him, but it also suggested the promise such a vessel presented—a promise sabotaged by the disinterest of *Bounty*'s owners in anything beyond a movie prop. He resented their consistent disregard for the rigorous attention to detail that her correct operation demanded. Yet his disappointment helped fire his attraction to the vision of a ship of his own, one like *Joe Lane,* whose likeness had stayed with him since that day a year earlier, sitting in Hawkins's living room overlooking the Benjamin River, when he had opened Howard Chapelle's magisterial volume and discovered the plans for the rakish revenue cutter. A schooner like the *Joe Lane* would be larger, more expensive, and more demanding than the straightforward Maine windjammers—but also, he came to believe, more exciting and more rewarding.

"You raise four sails and then you pick your nose," a favorite aphorism of his, explains Douglas's slight but very personal and particular disappointment with the handy fore-and-aft-rigged schooners of the tourist trade—disappointing, that is, to his kindled ambition and aesthetic. He preferred his one-day vessel to be larger, less pedestrian, more spirited—more like a clipper ship, recalling the thrilling history of a lean, fast, American breed of sailing vessels. After all, *Joe Lane* had been designed and built when American clippers stunned the world with their fast passages, especially between New York and San Francisco. Still, in January 1961, *Shenandoah* was not yet a plan, although Douglas's interest in a life under sail, with its challenges and rewards, had claimed a fixed place in his imagination.

Off and on until January 1962, when *Mary Day* was launched, Douglas helped out, and in the spring of 1962, after her launching, he sailed on her with Hawkins to Stonington, Maine, to be hauled so that her bottom could be cleaned and painted before the summer tourist season began. Here was an exquisite chance for a young man in the grip of a simmering idea for a sailing ship of his own to see firsthand what went into building a wooden sailing ship and to set his own idea of a schooner on the boil.

While Hawkins's schooner was building, Douglas delighted in the possibilities *Joe Lane* suggested. At the same time, the tangible, long-term commitment Hawkins had made over the years to the idea of the *Mary Day,* standing by until a moment arrived that made her possible, did not escape Douglas's notice. He also acknowledged to himself the value of Hawkins's and his family's considerable experience in the passenger schooner business before *Mary Day*. The evolution for Hawkins from the *Stephen Taber* to the *Alice Wentworth*—launched as the *Lizzie A. Tolles* in 1863—to the *Mary Day*, launched a century later, was a long, dedicated, careful, and eventful advance.

Being a gofer for Hawkins, Douglas recalls, "I had a nice time, got to know Harvey, got to know his crew. And the Coveside Inn was where I stayed later for a year and three months while I was building *Shenandoah*. So, looking back, it was a very clear progression of cause and effect."

And, in 1961, while *Mary Day* was building, another empty spot appeared in Gamage's lineup. For efficiency's sake, Gamage had to plan a year ahead of time, so Douglas gave the builder a check for $1,000 to claim that spot in line behind his friend's schooner. "As I look back on it," Douglas says, "I think I most likely wouldn't have got it in

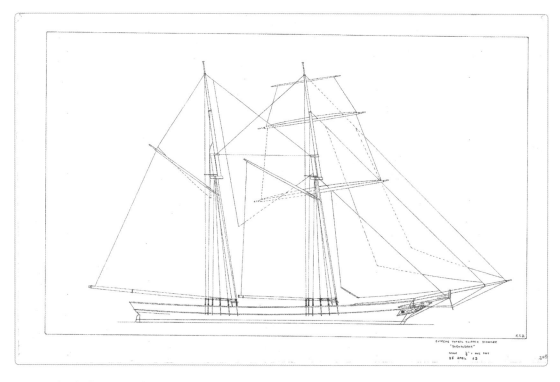

Douglas drafted most of *Shenandoah*'s hull and construction plans by November 1962, six months before her keel was laid, but he went on tinkering with *Joe Lane*'s sail plan—as drawn by Chapelle—after *Shenandoah*'s construction had begun. This April 1963 profile shows that Douglas has increased *Joe Lane*'s freeboard and begun to make changes to her rig, adding a foreboom to her loose-footed foresail. This iteration shows the staysail stay anchored to the bowsprit and the inner and outer jibstays anchored to the jibboom, a plan that resembles the way *Joe Lane*'s rig was secured. Douglas rejected this arrangement and would go on to change the head rig, ultimately anchoring the staysail stay to the stemhead, the inner jibstay to the bowsprit timber, and the outer jibstay to the end of the bowsprit, an arrangement that enormously strengthened support for the entire rig.

my head to do what I wanted to do if I hadn't been right there. But just then a spot came open, and it suddenly seemed like I might as well get in line with the other elephant. Because if you have a chance, hook onto his tail, and here we go."

"*Mary Day* was launched on January 15, 1962. I should know, because *Shenandoah* was launched on the 15th too, but it was February, two years later."

The difference between the decades-long unfolding achievement of Hawkins's deferred goal and the swift arc from notion to clearing acres of oaks from what remained of Gamage's woodlot for *Shenandoah*'s red oak keel, frames, and planking might suggest the common pitfalls of youthful ambition and intrepidity, but such an analysis would be wide of the mark. Douglas had made determined self-educational assaults on the history and mysteries of sailing, marine construction, and aviation. He pursued folks he met

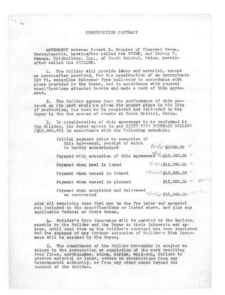

His experience of Harvey F. Gamage, businessman and shipbuilder, impressed Robert Douglas enormously. The Gamage enterprise was frill-less. There were only Gamage and a bookkeeper in the woodstove-heated office, with no secretary. Harvey was his own foreman. His shipwrights, some of them relatives and in-laws, worked a six-day week building two large vessels at a time in his huge shed. Douglas calls it "the most efficient operation" he has ever seen. The *Shenandoah* construction contract that Gamage hammered out on his typewriter described in two straightforward pages what Douglas could expect from the builder and what Gamage expected from him. The dates for construction to begin and finish were not specified. Instead, Gamage wrote, "The builder agrees that the performance of this contract on his part shall be given its proper place in his line of production, the boat to be completed and delivered to the buyer in the due course of events." There was a schedule of the payments required from Douglas as construction proceeded—ultimately totaling $65,000 "completed and delivered." On a third page was a terse, precise statement of construction specifications. A fourth and final page listed the materials that Douglas was to "furnish and install" in the months after *Shenandoah*'s launching, bringing Douglas's total outlay to about $170,000.

and liked who knew those pursuits intimately. Both sailing and flying are technically challenging, as are sailing ship design, drafting, and the smart, careful navigation of a demanding sailing vessel that is usually the largest in the small New England anchorages *Shenandoah* frequents. His aesthetic sensibilities are fervent, narrow but penetrating, informed and excited by examples of extraordinary craftsmanship. He is mechanically adept. He is frugal, except perhaps with historic marine artifacts and old boats he deems worthy of investment and salvation, and of course historic marine paintings. In Hawkins, Douglas had found a mentor and friend, similar to others earlier in his life—in school and in the Air Force. To all of these he paid absorbed attention.

Two advantages, rare to most young men determined to make a dream come true, helped make *Shenandoah* possible. First, Douglas had access to the financial resources necessary to realize his plans. "Dad was supportive," Douglas says. "He wasn't—I wouldn't say he was wildly out-of-his-mind supportive—but he supported me in every way that he could. He had money squirreled away in sort of a special account at one of his friend's banks in Chicago, and it was just enough to build the schooner.

"He thought it was a good thing, and I remember funny things that will stay in your head, like after my first season of carrying passengers and getting money for it—because the first season I gave back the deposits when the passengers came on board. Anyway, back in those days I was charging $150 a week for passengers, and I was paying each of my crew $40 per week. I think I had $10,000 left over after my first paying summer in 1965, and Dad said he thought it was a 'presentable sum . . . mildly impressive.' And that was pretty good."

Second, and perhaps more important, Douglas possessed an inborn determination to cut no corners, to do things correctly, to remain faithful to practices and traditions he was devoted to replicating and elevating aboard *Shenandoah*.

Gary Maynard, who grew up in Noank, Connecticut, met Douglas and *Shenandoah* as an eight-year-old when he saw *Shenandoah* come up the Mystic River to the Seaport Museum and was enchanted by the sight. He eventually rose in rank aboard *Shenandoah* from galley boy to deckhand to boatswain to mate, absorbing Douglas's leadership style. "It was the discipline," he says. "Maintenance, especially. And then the discipline of keeping a clean vessel and caring. Like we literally used to have foxtails and sponges, not brooms and mops. Because you had to get on your knees and be close to the dirt when you were cleaning the cabin sole. And there was a tremendous pride in that aboard *Shenandoah*.

"Stowing the sails? Nobody stows the sails like she does. Everything was always like—the alignment of the yards. Everything was like people really, really cared. And that all comes from Bob. I mean, he used to stand at the wheel—it's just so hard for people to get this now—he'd stand there with his binoculars, and he'd look at the rig and say, 'The seventeenth batten on the main is down an inch on the aft end.' And you'd have to go up and re-seize it. It was hard-core. But it was great for a guy like me that really dug it.

"But you were always on the go. You had every other Sunday off. And you had one night off a week, I think, from watch. So you were tired, because you were up for night watch all but one night, I think, maybe two. And you worked constantly, though sometimes you had mornings off if you were in port. We would split the crew, and some would stay on for maintenance work.

"So it was like an old-time ship. You repaired sails, you replaced running rigging, you maintained blocks, you did paint touch-up. Not just polishing

As was his longstanding practice, Gamage cut the oak that became *Shenandoah* from a woodlot he owned a few miles from the boatyard. The yard's boatbuilders felled the trees, milled them, and took patterns of the frames and other parts of the vessel into the woods to look for the natural shapes that would best serve each construction element. *Shenandoah*'s construction exhausted the woodlot.

brass, but you did everything. The only thing we didn't do? We didn't steer or navigate. Nobody except Bob ever steered or navigated, including the mate. Just wasn't part of it. And we didn't do any carpentry.

"And it's a wonderful thing to be able, if you care, to do it all right. To be given the authority to do it right. And be given the expectation to do it right. The reward was the vessel. And that's very nineteenth century."

Mary Day's launching on January 15, 1962, marked the actual beginning of the partnership between Douglas and the ship that had begun as *Joe Lane* and would become *Shenandoah*. There was a lot to be done. *Joe Lane* had enthralled him from the moment he came across her description and plans in Chapelle's book, but he wanted to make significant changes. Below decks, *Joe Lane* had lacked standing headroom except perhaps aft. Even on calm sailing days, it is impossible to imagine thirty paying passengers cheerfully spending vacation time doubled over below decks and banging their heads on deck beams. And in stiff sailing conditions, when *Joe Lane*'s lee rail and a good deal of the lee deck would likely be underwater, her decks would have been a dangerous place for a paying passenger or anyone, really, to pass. Douglas raised the deck in *Joe Lane*'s plans about one and a half feet by extending the double-sawn red oak frames while leaving *Joe Lane*'s bulwarks unchanged.

Of course, as he raised the deck, the bulwarks, though themselves no taller, rose too. In her 1851 plans, the only surviving plans for *Joe Lane*'s cutter class, her stern was rounded in plan view. It remained so as it rose a foot and a half on Douglas's drafting board. Likewise, at the bow, Douglas's changes lengthened her modestly.

Douglas made small changes to *Joe Lane*'s diagonals aft of midships to more closely imitate their shape forward. In total, Douglas's modifications, chiefly due to the increase in deck height, resulted in a vessel that was very slightly longer than *Joe Lane*. *Shenandoah*'s displacement of 170 tons was also somewhat greater than her forebear. The beam remained 23 feet, but her draft increased to 10 feet 6 inches from 9 feet 7½ inches.

Douglas was particularly keen to revise *Joe Lane*'s head rig, to strengthen what is the main support for the sail plan. "*Joe Lane* had a single headstay that went to the end of the bowsprit, which I don't like. That's a bad plan. That's what lost the whole rig out of the *Pride of Baltimore*," he says. "You need more than just one stay supporting the whole rig of the boat." In his revision, he anchored the outer jibstay to the end of the jibboom, the inner jibstay to the bowsprit timber, and the headstay on which the jib staysail (sometimes called the jumbo) was set to the gammon iron at the stemhead. *Shenandoah*'s rig and her 7,000 square feet of sail were supported by three wire stays.

He also altered *Joe Lane*'s foresail. "The foresail on the *Joe Lane* was loose-footed à la *Pride of Baltimore,* and sheeted like a jib," Douglas explains. "You'd have to have two handy billies, one on either side of the mast, to clap on the sheet, just like a big jib. *Shenandoah*'s got a foreboom and gaff instead. For *Joe Lane* they wanted more sail area—you got so much more horsepower, I guess—and thought that the complications wouldn't make too much difference. But that's a big pain in the ass. When tacking you have to ease the old lee tackle and sheet in with the other handy billy on the new lee side to get the sail sheeted tight. That's a major difference."

Working from plans obtained from Howard Chapelle himself, then curator of the National Watercraft Collection at the Smithsonian, Douglas conceived his changes to *Joe Lane*, drafting the revised plans himself in the southeast-facing corner room of his Vineyard Haven house. The house had been built in 1802 off Main Street, overlooking Vineyard Haven Harbor. He had bought it in January 1961—signing the papers while still in Tahiti—and as he drafted his plans for *Shenandoah*, workmen were rebuilding the house. Most of the plans he created are dated November 1962.

While he was working at his drafting table—a hollow veneered door he'd bought at the local lumberyard and supported by two sawhorses—Douglas had a visitor. Ike Norton of Edgartown, whose family had been prominent in the off-shore fishing business and in town affairs, knocked on the front door to see if he could persuade Douglas to relinquish his reserved place in the Gamage yard's lineup. Norton had a dragger he wanted to build, and he knew that Douglas had a great deal of work to do before construction could begin on his schooner.

Douglas declined Norton's offer, so Norton and his partner, Jens Isaksen, got in line for the next opening. As it happened, their dragger *Jane and Ursula*, which Douglas often describes as *Shenandoah*'s

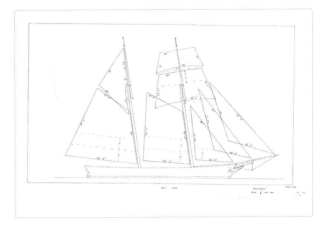

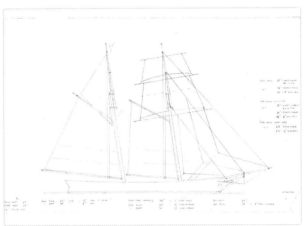

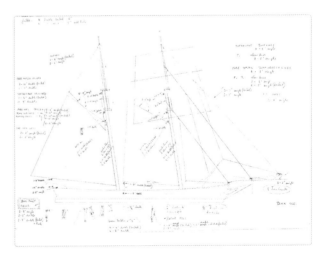

These *Shenandoah* sail and rigging plans are dated March 2, 1964, two weeks after her launching. The forestaysail stay now lands at the stemhead, the inner jib is anchored at the bowsprit timber, and the outer jibstay runs to the end of the jibboom.

sister ship, was built next to *Shenandoah* and launched a little later than *Shenandoah* in 1964. She was 86 feet long, 168 gross tons, and 10 feet 9 inches deep. The construction of *Jane and Ursula*'s round stern, and indeed the entire vessel, Douglas often points out, was identical to *Shenandoah*'s. Fishermen looking to build big offshore draggers were regular customers of Gamage, and he had tried-and-true construction methods, materials, and scantlings. Gamage employed his system of rugged construction for fishing boats and topsail schooners alike. "*Shenandoah*'s structure, she's one of his draggers, you know. Built just like it. She was built as heavy as any of his biggest draggers. And some of the draggers were bigger," Douglas says. *Jane and Ursula* was lost at sea in 1973.

Shenandoah's keel was laid on May 1, 1963. By then, Douglas had finished modifying *Joe Lane*'s body plan, drawn a deck plan and a construction plan, and tried twelve versions of an interior accommodations plan before he was finally satisfied. The interior and deck plans went hand in hand, the former dictating the latter. Douglas settled in at the Coveside Inn once again. Elaine Jensen, who ran the place with her husband, took good care of him, charging four dollars a day for the room, three meals, and laundry. At the shipyard he made himself comfortable in Harvey Gamage's spare third-floor office.

Looking aft, with the sternpost visible in the right background. Shipwrights are erecting the framing stock and hand-shaping it with adzes. The finished frames will be 11 inches thick at the keel and taper to 6 inches at deck level, well above this photograph's field of view.

"He had a beautiful shop, a beautiful office with a big Fairy Oak woodstove and an endless supply of wood to burn. I had to be there. I was just taking care of mail, and I had to think about getting a crew together. I had to design the rig and its detail and get that all together with Pigeon Hollow Spar Company in East Boston, which built the spars, and with Henry Bohndell in Rockport, who did all the wire work and splicing.

"The first month when construction began, I think I spent most of my time with a big slick I had, a big chisel, getting rid of as much of the sapwood as I could off the frame stock, because Harvey didn't care about that, and sapwood gets rotten quicker than anything. All the oak that was going in the boat was lying at the head of the building shed. I don't think I missed a weekday in the year

Shenandoah's sternpost and the deadwood built up in front of and alongside it are visible in this photograph. The underpinnings of the schooner's lovely circular stern would be almost solid oak up to deck level.

and three months until we left the yard. I'd come home now and again on the weekends.

"Harvey and I got along real good. The only problem I had with him was with the deck planking on the after house, which I drew as three-inch planking on the plans, just like the main deck. I did that because on the deckhouse, up and away from the water sloshing around and not getting as much moisture as the main deck might get, you need something that's got more stability to it so the seams won't open. But Harvey said, 'You don't need that'—I don't know, maybe he didn't have the wood—so the damn deck on the house is inch-and-a-half, and it was never tight."

Because *Shenandoah* was 100 feet long,

Looking aft. Because the stern circle is framed differently from the rest of the schooner and built up with deadwood to deck level, there are no frame heads standing up there as they do along *Shenandoah*'s sides.

as *Joe Lane* had been, and because her rig was largely the same, rigging details that Donald MacKay had documented and published on the size and shape of spars for such a vessel

Looking forward over *Shenandoah*'s deck framing. The prominent deckbeam in the foreground separates what will be the captain's cabin, farthest aft, from the galley and several passenger cabins.

"gave me the shape of all the spars on the boat. Her masts were 20 inches at the deck and 16 inches at the cap iron, just like McKay had prescribed in his book, which was written in the 1850s. The rig is the same. You'll see a plan drawing of *Joe Lane*, it looks like

As construction nears completion, a worker caulks the seam above the garboard or bottom-most plank.

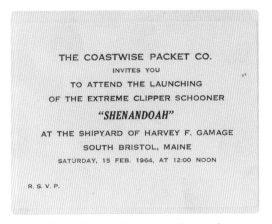

THE COASTWISE PACKET CO.

INVITES YOU

TO ATTEND THE LAUNCHING

OF THE EXTREME CLIPPER SCHOONER

"SHENANDOAH"

AT THE SHIPYARD OF HARVEY F. GAMAGE
SOUTH BRISTOL, MAINE
SATURDAY, 15 FEB. 1964, AT 12:00 NOON

R. S. V. P.

Launching day drew near at last, and invitations were printed and sent.

Launching day. The projections at the rail on each side of Shenandoah's bow are the catheads. There are port and starboard anchors. When an anchor is retrieved it is first hauled up to the cathead and secured, then the anchor's flukes are drawn up and caught on the rail a few feet aft of the cathead and lashed in place.

The McPherson Pine Tree Band—with eight pipers, three drummers, and a drum major—sent Shenandoah rushing into her element to the tune of "Road to the Isles." "I'll never forget the fine noise they made, playing in the big wooden shed," Douglas says.

Shenandoah without the freeboard. Shenandoah has got the kind of freeboard that makes sense for a boat that size."

Beauty is key to Douglas's appreciation of a sailing vessel, and a motor vessel too, truth be told. He believes beauty—like construction, materials, speed, and the power of its rig—is indispensable in judging the quality of a sailing vessel, and a boat's sheer is key to her beauty.

"I said to Harvey, 'You're going to have to give me the time necessary, so I am satisfied with the sheer.' He said, 'Okay, no problem. Just don't get in my way, you know?' Unfortunately, the starboard side was very close to the big posts in the middle of this big building shed, and Harvey had a hard time getting an unobstructed view of the starboard side, which wound up being

Gathering speed as she headed down the ways, rudder centered, bedecked with bunting and carrying a cargo of VIPs, *Shenandoah* slid into the Damariscotta River at high tide. Cheers and bagpipe music drowned out her splash. Visible above the stern rail and wheel is the gallows frame from which the yawl boat will hang.

very crooked in one place. So, I was there, playing around, and he's got the stern circle down, and the sheer strake is on it, and it's supposed to be a smooth, gentle curve from the top of the stern circle to the top of the sheer strake, but instead you've got something that looks nuts.

Moored at the Gamage dock. The gathering on *Shenandoah*'s deck includes (foreground from right to left) designer Murray Peterson; Hugh Boyd, a crewman on *Bounty* with Douglas; designer-boatbuilder Pete Culler (bright checked shirt); Robert Douglas (dark checked shirt); Douglas's longtime friend Bernie Holzer (to Douglas's left); and (beyond Holzer), Douglas's brother David.

Launched without spars, inside ballast, and most of her equipment and fixtures, *Shenandoah* floated well above her marks.

When Harvey Gamage died in the fall of 1976, Douglas gathered a postseason crew and sailed *Shenandoah* to South Bristol to honor the shipbuilder. On that trip *Shenandoah* spent a night at anchor in Pulpit Harbor on North Haven Island.

"When *Mary Day* was building, Buds had brought a Skil electric plane to the yard. Until then, Harvey had no power planes in his yard. You chopped down stanchions and did everything with an adze. Well, Harvey had seen that plane and realized he could make some hay with a tool like that, and the next day he had a dozen of them. So, I found a nice stick of wood to use as a straightedge, and I put it down on the line between the top of the sheer strake and the top of the stern circle, and it ended up rocking back and forth, obviously wrong, and I went at it with the electric plane. Harvey said, 'You don't care how much time you waste, do you?' And I said, 'Don't worry, Harvey, when this boat goes down the river, you're never going to see her again.' I was a little upset. 'It's going to be my major enterprise forever,' I told him, 'and I think it's worth the time to make this look right.'

"Anyway, I got the last laugh later, because the *Jane and Ursula* got built alongside me, and she had the same stern and the same problem. And when I saw Harvey over there with a straightedge and a Skil plane, I saw my chance to say, 'Harvey, can't suit you, huh? Oh, you're too fussy,' but I let it pass."

Douglas's great friend Bernie Holzer, who had gone to sea at age 16 on Great Lakes freighters and later became a Vineyard resident and a regular guest in Douglas's Vineyard Haven kitchen, set the colors up on a stick as *Shenandoah* slid into the water on February 15, 1964. As she began her descent into her natural element, Douglas's father shattered a champagne bottle on her stem. *Shenandoah* was following *Mary Day* (1962) out of Gamage's shed. The Hudson River sloop *Clearwater* (1969) and the passenger schooners *Bill of Rights* (1971) and *Harvey Gamage* (1973) would follow *Shenandoah*.

Harvey Gamage was in his mid-sixties when he built Douglas's schooner, about the same age as Douglas's father. Gamage died in 1976. "We went down that fall," Douglas remembers. "We had enough crew that weren't going back to school, so we could sail the boat there. We got there about a week after he died and tied up at the yard."

Chapter Seven

Adrift in Bureaucratic Seas

DOUGLAS'S FIRST BRUSH with federal regulations had to do with gross tonnage, a volumetric measurement of the space inside a vessel that, broadly defined, is used to do its business. The US Treasury Department does the measuring, but permission to operate under a particular set of categories is granted by the Coast Guard. In 1956, Congress, in response to the 1955 sinking of the Chesapeake Bay schooner *Levin J. Marvel* during Hurricane Connie, had expanded the responsibility of the Coast Guard for inspecting and licensing passenger-carrying vessels to include those as small as 100 gross tons. Lives had been lost in the sinking of the soft old schooner, anchored in an exposed location when the storm blew through the Chesapeake. She fell apart at anchor. The rules governing the Coast Guard's inspection work with these smaller vessels were not completed until 1968, but in 1963 Douglas did not expect that to matter.

He intended to sail *Shenandoah* under Subchapter T, for vessels of less than 100 gross tons that carry 150 or fewer passengers or have overnight accommodations for 49 or fewer passengers. (Today, Coast Guard approval is required for all passenger-carrying vessels, no matter the tonnage.)

Douglas's own calculations found *Shenandoah*'s gross tonnage to be under the limit, but the Treasury official from the US Customs office in Rockland, Maine, arrived at a higher number. Several months' delay of construction was consumed, first in debate over the competing calculations and then in devising a workable plan to reduce the officially measured tonnage. The eventual solution was to add 4½-inch-wide oak floors on one futtock on every other frame. This reduced the usable interior space, which solved the problem.

In April 1963, as construction was about to begin, Douglas submitted *Shenandoah*'s plans to the Coast Guard's Officer in Charge of Marine Inspection (OCMI) at Portland, Maine, who sent the plans on to the Coast Guard in Boston, who returned them to Portland. Over time, Coast Guard officials in Maine, Boston, New York, and Washington participated in the review and the final decision on whether *Shenandoah* was safe enough to carry paying passengers.

The decision on *Shenandoah*'s certification was particularly troublesome for the Coast Guard, which was forced to confront its own previously lenient standards—common for years by then—for licensing the vessels of the Maine windjammer fleet. The Coast Guard OCMI for Portland had taken on the certification of the several vessels operating in his district, rarely if ever asking for guidance from merchant marine technical authorities up the chain of command or in other sectors. But only two vessels in the Maine fleet were as large as *Shenandoah* was to be, and none was an "extreme clipper schooner"—that is, a vessel characterized by fine lines, light displacement, and a powerful sail plan. Douglas came to regret this description of his vessel in communications with Coast Guard personnel and in promotional materials. He worried that the label—a source of pride for him—alarmed the permitting authorities and put them on their guard. None of the schooners in the Maine windjammer fleet had clipper hull forms, and none set square sails or even had topmasts from which gaff topsails could be set. Most at that time were living their second or third lives, aged veterans of the freight trade, repurposed for carrying passengers. *Shenandoah*, sleek and speedy looking, her raked masts reaching 94 feet above the water and carrying three jibs, a square topsail and topgallant on the foremast, and a main gaff topsail besides her two lowers, was something new and worrisome.

In August 1963, Harvey Gamage wrote to the Coast Guard in support of Douglas's application for a license to operate his schooner with paying passengers. Gamage described the sturdy construction for which his company was known, asserting that *Shenandoah*'s construction was at least as durable as the minesweepers and draggers he built, and in some ways more so. "I have no hesitation in stating that the structural strength and design of Mr. Douglas's vessel far exceeds the requirement for her intended service," he wrote.

In the Maine fleet the former cargo carriers had been rebuilt in part or extensively and refitted with cabins for passengers. Many were centerboard vessels and had no outside ballast. Only *Mary Day*, launched two years before *Shenandoah*, had been purpose-built for the passenger trade. Her centerboard was on the vessel's centerline, varying from what had been the common practice, which placed the centerboard to one side or the other of the keel, requiring the nearby mainmast to be stepped off the centerline of the vessel. *Mary Day*'s centerboard dropped through the keel on the centerline. Hawkins's design also called for a six-ton cast-iron shoe along her keel that had the effect of supplying some outside ballast and compensating for any strength sacrificed by lowering the centerboard through the keel. Most of the veterans were grandfathered into their licenses, and none, including *Mary Day*, had been subjected to incline experiments to test their stability.

The complications that ensued over Douglas's license application had never arisen in the Coast Guard's treatment of other sailing passenger schooners based in Maine. "I had seen *Mary Day* get built from A to Z. I saw Buds drawing lines on a piece of paper. I was there during the construction. I was there at the launching. I was there for the first sail. I was there for the first week's cruise. I had been as tightly involved with the vessel's building as if I had been Hawkins. And there was nothing from the Coast Guard to do with stability," Douglas says.

Coast Guard technical offices from Maine to Washington, DC were unaccustomed to being called into service to rule on certifying members of the Maine fleet. As Coast Guard Commander Richard Bryant Brooks, a staff officer in the technical division at Washington headquarters, explained, "No commercial sailing vessel with such a complex sail arrangement and unusual hull design had ever been certificated by the Coast Guard for oceangoing passenger service."

On the question of what stability standards to apply, the bargaining between Douglas and the Coast Guard began in earnest with a July 7, 1964, communication from the New York technical office that "a 90-degree range of stability must be obtained" by *Shenandoah* if she were to be licensed. In other words, she must be able to recover from a 90-degree knockdown. After all, to the Coast Guard she was an anomaly, larger than the schooners that had come before her seeking Subchapter T certification, and with a taller rig. Douglas appealed this demand, and his legal counsel told a December 17, 1964, appeal hearing that, "As a matter of fact, from the very beginning [of the negotiations] and to this day, the 90-degree range criterion, if you will, has never been mentioned since. It was apparently no longer considered a valid criterion." The Coast Guard later described the "must be obtained" 90-degree recovery requirement as an "initial position."

Douglas's July appeal also rejected other requirements proposed by the Coast Guard during months of bargaining. These included heavily increasing her ballast—she had already taken on 17 tons of lead before leaving Gamage's yard and added another 20 tons under the floorboards later in the summer of 1964 at Woods Hole, coinciding with a week when Buds Hawkins and his family were invited guests for a week's cruise. William Bunting, *Shenandoah*'s bosun, fresh from his experience in the sinking of the school ship *Albatross*, thought *Shenandoah* seemed tender and in need of more ballast. Tony Higgins, the mate, had a similar impression and also thought that *Shenandoah* needed to be more heavily ballasted to help her carry her way through a tack.

The Coast Guard also asked that Douglas eliminate one of *Shenandoah*'s three jibs, the main gaff topsail, the square topsail, and the topgallant from her rig. In effect this would have transformed *Shenandoah*'s rig from the nineteenth-century topsail schooner *Joe Lane*—which had served the United States Revenue Marine for fifteen years on both coasts of the young country—into an enfeebled, bald-headed fore-and-aft schooner of the type common in the Maine windjammer fleet. Douglas said that if he had to scandalize *Shenandoah*'s rig as the Coast Guard proposed, "She wouldn't even tack."

Douglas resisted every one of these demands and eventually filed an unsuccessful lawsuit against the Coast Guard to recover the untallied thousands of dollars he had to spend to get his new vessel licensed. Because *Shenandoah* was not certified for paying passengers in summer 1964, his first season of operations was lost, and his out-of-pocket costs totaled approximately $50,000, not including legal and consulting costs.

In August 1967, Coast Guard Commander Brooks, a staff officer in the technical division at Washington headquarters, was deposed in the course of Douglas's lawsuit. By then, *Shenandoah* had operated successfully for most of four seasons—the first with passengers whose reservations were honored though their fees were refunded. Despite its onerous initial requirements and limitations, the Coast Guard had eventually permitted her pretty much as designed, with modest requirements consistent with Douglas's careful practice.

Douglas's counsel in the unsuccessful lawsuit—as in the earlier, successful appeal hearings—was Daniel Featherstone Jr., of Boston's Choate, Hall and Stewart, a well-known and highly regarded defense attorney who was described in his June 1996 *Boston Globe* obituary as "something to behold when he was on his game." He was 67 when he died. Featherstone asked Commander Brooks, "Isn't it true that, at that time in May of 1963, there was no regulation specifically setting out a standard for stability for sailing vessels?" Brooks's responses help explain why *Shenandoah* was such a problem for the Coast Guard:

> Brooks: "At the time, Subchapter T did not specifically deal with stability."
> Featherstone: "Am I not also correct that there is [no such regulation] now?"
> Brooks: "You are correct."

Not only was *Shenandoah* an outlier among the windjammer schooners inspected by OCMI Portland, Douglas's application initiated a fluctuating debate and negotiation over a variety of stability indicators put forward by competing naval architects. Each side measured the same distances, weights, and heights, but one calculated the pressure per square foot of a 30-mile-per-hour wind (26 knots) on *Shenandoah*'s sails, while the other calculated the pressure generated by a 30-knot wind (35 miles per hour). They debated how much stability was needed and how much lead ballast should be added to reach it. They performed two supervised incline experiments, one at South Bristol, before she left the Gamage yard for Martha's Vineyard and sailed into a 40-knot northeaster, and the other in Vineyard Haven Harbor, after 20 more tons of ballast had been set by hand into every possible cranny under *Shenandoah*'s floorboards.

Of course the loss of the 92-foot *Albatross* on May 2, 1961, cast a shadow over the question of what conditions should be imposed on *Shenandoah*'s operation. Built in Holland in 1920 as a schooner-rigged pilot ship for service in the always rambunctious North Sea, she was rerigged as a brigantine in 1954 by her new owner, the writer Ernest Gann. *Tabor Boy*, the school ship of Tabor Academy in Marion, Massachusetts, is a similar design to *Albatross*, likewise built in Holland for North Sea pilot service. Christopher B. Sheldon bought *Albatross* in 1959, becoming her captain and, with his wife, Dr. Alice Sheldon, the creator of the Ocean Academy in Darien, Connecticut. *Albatross* took 14 or 15 students on sailing educational journeys in the Caribbean and Eastern Pacific. She was lost in the Gulf of Mexico when a powerful microburst struck suddenly and laid her immediately on her side. She filled with water and sank within 60 seconds, according to reports. Of the eighteen aboard, six were lost, including Dr. Sheldon. The *Albatross* was 97 gross registered tons, similar to *Shenandoah*, and her loss added more urgency to the Coast Guard's deliberations.

Among the strange twists and turns in the effort to get *Shenandoah* certified, perhaps the greatest unforeseen irony was the appearance of Howard I. Chapelle among the opposition. It was Chapelle's *History of American Sailing Ships* that had introduced Douglas to the revenue cutter *Joe Lane*, *Shenandoah*'s avatar. Chapelle had furnished Douglas with *Joe Lane*'s plans, which were preserved in the Watercraft Collection of the Smithsonian Institution, where Chapelle worked, and he was among the earliest to know of Douglas's plan to build *Shenandoah* and to carry passengers under sail. But the Coast Guard consulted with Chapelle as it formed its preliminary view of the prospects for *Shenandoah*'s safe operation, and he appeared as a witness for the Coast Guard at the December 1964 hearing of Douglas's appeal.

Deepening the irony, the United States Revenue Marine—which had built *Joe Lane* and five other vessels of the same design—had merged with the United States Life Saving Service in 1915 to form the US Coast Guard. In the idiom of the twenty-first century, *Joe Lane* and *Shenandoah* have shared DNA.

At the hearing, Chapelle, who died at age 74 in 1975, took issue with the stability numbers of several of the vessels with which Douglas's naval architects compared *Shenandoah* in order to place her stability in what Evers Burtner, associate professor of naval architecture and marine engineering at the Massachusetts Institute of Technology, called "the ballpark, to use a slang phrase." Chapelle relentlessly criticized the results on grounds that the comparison vessels were of greater displacement and different models than *Shenandoah* and represented a "different set of proportions" with greater stability as designed. He was an unwavering critic of *Shenandoah*'s hull form and rig and what he described as the difficulty of ballasting her sufficiently to lower her center of gravity. Chapelle had himself designed the successful topsail schooner *Caribee*, a clipper schooner model setting a triangular course on the foremast. She was one of the vessels used in comparisons of hull form and rig in the *Shenandoah* licensing debate.

Curiously, when *Shenandoah* was under construction at Gamage's yard in 1963, Douglas, who spent nearly every working day at the shipyard, made a rare excursion. "I was present every day except three," Douglas says, "when I took a trip to Miami to check out a boat that was for sale. It was a remarkable coincidence that the vessel was *Caribee*, designed by Chapelle and built by his partner William Robinson in Ipswich, Massachusetts, in 1938."

Chapelle testified that the history of schooners carrying square sails was replete with knockdowns and sinkings because the gear to manage heavy yards made it difficult and time-consuming to get sail off in a hurry. This applied even to the most capable vessels commanded and crewed by experienced mariners, he said. He favored lighter gear that was designed to lower yards quickly to the deck without sending someone aloft to assist. *Shenandoah* has three yards: a course to spread the foot of the topsail above; a topsail yard that also spreads the foot of the topgallant above it, and highest aloft, the topgallant yard. To set each square sail, the gasket that holds the furled sail must be thrown off, along with the clew lines and buntlines, which must be overhauled. Then the yard is hoisted, the sail is sheeted in, and finally the yard is braced to serve the compass course the vessel is steering relative to the wind direction. All this must be done in reverse order to furl the topsails. The spars are heavy and would be impossible to lower quickly to the deck in an emergency.

Could the skill and experience of the master and crew of such a vessel make it safe? "There isn't any such thing as completely safe, of course, but there must be a degree of safety that we can establish for a basis of comparison," Chapelle told the hearing. "For every vessel that will right herself up to 90 degrees, you will find plenty of records of vessels that could not, but it does not prove anything."

Chapelle argued strenuously that although the clipper-type hull and rig found in *Shenandoah* and in some late-nineteenth-century fishing schooners promised speed, "the inability to stow ballast low enough . . . was the real cause of the danger of these vessels and the cause of a great many of these losses, capsizing or running off, and many of the boats went down."

Nevertheless, Chapelle had celebrated the revenue cutter designs in his *History of American Sailing Ships*. He wrote:

> The spirit and traditions of the present Coast Guard were founded in the slippery little revenue schooners of the days of sail. These rakish topsail schooners, slashing through the heavy seas of a winter's gale were the first to express the motto of the present service, *Semper Paratus* (Always Ready).
>
> The design of the sailing revenue cutter was a problem similar in most respects to that of the design of a privateer. The cutters could be lightly armed and manned, but speed was an absolute necessity if the vessels were to be successful. Since the cutters must spend much of their lives at sea, the need for reasonable seaworthiness was obvious. In order to catch smugglers and other lawbreakers, weatherliness was also very important. On many stations a shoal-draft vessel would be most efficient, excessive draft in any case was undesirable. As cutters were not expected to fight regular naval engagements, the bulwarks could be light or omitted entirely.

"*Joe Lane* couldn't have been too bad a boat. She went around the Horn, and she was stationed at Port Townsend in Washington state for ten years," Douglas concluded.

Naval architects studying the history of such ships on Douglas's behalf argued that *Shenandoah*'s shape above the waterline at the flaring bow and below the waterline, where ballasting could be concentrated, improved on the lines of the fishing schooners, whose designs also emphasized speed. This debate was never resolved. Instead, Douglas explained as the hearing concluded, "As you all know, I operated the vessel all summer long in 1964. The main reason I did this was to be able to show everybody concerned that she was adequate to do the job. She handled well, and we ran into no difficulties of any kind between South Bristol, Maine, and Block Island, Rhode Island. We need to go on available material, namely the operation of the boat. . . . So, if we can keep vessels that have done the job in mind—and, as Mr. Chapelle mentioned, he can't design a vessel that is foolproof—our whole problem here, as we all are well aware, I am sure, is to come up with a workable requirement for safety."

In the spring of 1965, *Shenandoah* was hauled out at Norlantic Diesel (later D. N. Kelly Shipyard), in Fairhaven, Massachusetts, for annual maintenance before beginning her second season of operation. North of her on the yard's other railway was the *Alice Wentworth*, built in the nineteenth century and finally being retired from service and refitted as an attraction at Anthony Athanas's Pier Four restaurant in Boston. West of *Shenandoah*, moored at the shipyard's dock, was the schooner *Ernestina*, just arrived from the Canary Islands with a deck cargo of livestock, sundry passengers, and crew. A schooner of many lives, in 2021 *Ernestina* was completing a well-funded and wonderfully executed reconstruction as a school ship to be based at the Massachusetts Maritime Academy on the Cape Cod Canal and in New Bedford, Massachusetts.

While Douglas and his crew did their maintenance work, they had a visitor. Lou Parker, the Coast Guard officer in charge of marine inspection (OCMI) for the Boston district, came to make *Shenandoah*'s annual inspection and to give Douglas the certificate he had pursued for a year. The certificate restricted Douglas to operating coastwise between Schoodic Peninsula in Maine and Sandy Hook, New Jersey. It required Douglas to raise the thresholds to each of the two athwartship companionways in the vessel's deckhouse one foot, and to furl the fore topgallant, fore topsail, and main gaff topsail when the wind exceeded 15 knots. Douglas may have thought these restrictions unnecessary, but he has adhered to them since that spring day more than a half century ago, operating without incident up and down the coast.

Chapter Eight

In Business

To this day, Robert Douglas smarts at the expensive pummeling he took during the year between *Shenandoah's* launching on February 15, 1964, when his delight in his spanking new vessel was unrestrained, and her first week with paying customers aboard in June 1965, when every element of his life's consuming idea had at last been realized. For him, the villain of this piece was and remains the Coast Guard.

"Maybe you should be nice to everybody. I don't know," he says. "My Coast Guard friends, well, they were and still are my basic problem and have been right along. They precluded my operation for my first year because we didn't have the right stability. They hadn't yet codified a stability standard you could build a boat to, and they wouldn't for another ten years. It took them ten years after they screwed me up, and if it hadn't been for Lou Parker, the Portland District inspector, I'm sure I would never have had a license. He's the guy who took the bull by the horns, because his dad had been in the schooner business. His father had come from Nova Scotia, and Lou used to spend summers in Maine when he wasn't in school."

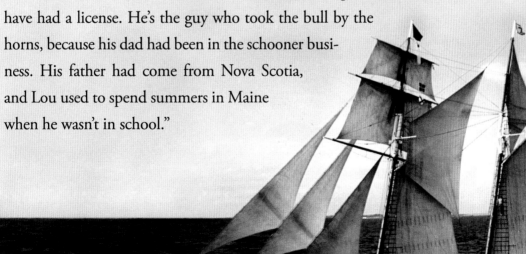

Not surprisingly, the second chapter of Jack London's *Cruise of the Snark*—a favorite of Douglas's youth along with Robert Louis Stevenson's *Treasure Island* and John Masefield's *Jim Davis*—is the one Douglas remembers best and often invokes. He especially likes its title, "The Inconceivable and Monstrous." It speaks to him, as it must to anyone who has polished a dream to a sweet luster only to watch as the execution of the plan drains or at least dulls its gleaming promise. He had found himself in the grip of New England maritime life; he had found encouragement and example in Havilah Hawkins; he had moved quickly to shape his idea on the drafting board and to make it real. All that had worked out very well, but then the "inconceivable and monstrous" intervened.

In a frisky southwesterly, *Shenandoah* hurries along on five lowers off West Chop, Martha's Vineyard, her main gaff topsail and square sails smartly furled to their spars.

Building the *Snark*, London had made a no-detail-overlooked, no-expenses-spared plan, yet nothing went smoothly. "Then there was the matter of delay," he wrote. "I dealt with forty-seven different kinds of union men and with one hundred and fifteen different firms":

> And not one union man and not one firm of all the union men and all the firms ever delivered anything at the time agreed upon, nor ever was on time for anything except pay-day and bill-collection. Men pledged me their immortal souls that they would deliver a certain thing on a certain date; as a rule, after such pledging, they rarely exceeded being three months late in delivery. And so it went.
>
> And in the end we sailed away, on Tuesday morning, April 23, 1907 [one year after the planned departure]. We started rather lame, I confess. We had to hoist the anchor by hand, because the power transmission was a wreck. Also, what remained of our seventy-horsepower engine was lashed down for ballast on the bottom of the *Snark*. But what of such things? They could be fixed in Honolulu, and in the meantime think of the magnificent rest of the boat! It is true, the engine in the launch wouldn't run, and the lifeboat leaked like a sieve; but then they weren't the *Snark*; they were mere appurtenances. The things that counted were the watertight bulkheads, the solid planking without butts, the bathroom devices—they were the *Snark*. And then there was, greatest of all, that noble, wind-punching bow.

Practical and deliberate as London had been in planning his round-the-world adventure, it was the beauty and authority of his schooner's handsome bow, for him a talisman of sorts, that kept him and his wife on course.

To be sure, none of London's inconceivable and monstrous problems were the same as Douglas's. The execution of Douglas's plan, once materialized in his thinking, was remarkably swift and flawless, at least until *Shenandoah* was launched. The subsequent year he and she spent in irons might have ended calamitously with no license to operate, but it did not. Instead, there came a moment in June 1965 when Douglas took *Shenandoah*'s helm for the first time with paying passengers on board. One can imagine him, detached and absorbed, while passengers loafed on the deckhouse in front of him, puzzling over his quiet manner and perhaps judging him to be unapproachable though he was not, as his creation, her sheets started, sped toward Cross Rip on the way to Nantucket.

Bob Douglas at *Shenandoah's* helm in the early years.

Gary Maynard was only eight years old when he caught a glimpse of *Shenandoah* and succumbed. "I remember *Shenandoah* from an early age," he recalled, "and I remember her coming up the Sound from Watch Hill, I think just under the topsails. We were in a little Noank sloop called the *Jeff Brown,* and they passed us. And I remember that quarterboard, this enormously long black-and-white quarterboard, saying *Shenandoah.* And I remember the guy leaning over the davits watching us, because *Jeff Brown* was a really pretty little boat."

Anyone who sailed aboard *Shenandoah*—a passenger, a fresh member of the crew, or an old hand—will have seen what Maynard remembers. Underway or at anchor, often with binoculars, Douglas examined the seascape, the landscape, the rig, the run of the current, the set of his sails, the wind, the sky, the weather on the horizon, the passing vessels. Over the years, he observed and indexed what he saw for immediate retrieval. The scope of his interest was vast but focused. His operating range over half a century was generally between Nantucket Sound and Long Island Sound, and he was intimate with the currents, the weather, the wind directions, the vessels, and what anchorages were possible with the conditions prevailing on any sailing day. He may have set out for Padanaram on a particular day, but a shifting or softening wind found him instead at Kettle Cove on the north shore of Naushon Island that evening.

When she slipped down Harvey Gamage's ways, *Shenandoah* was a mystery. Douglas had expectations of her handling qualities, her speed, and how weatherly she would be, but he could not know for sure. She reminded him of how unrealistic the Coast Guard had been early in the negotiations, when they proposed to require him to carry only the four lowers—main, foresail, staysail, and jib. With the loss of sail area, and especially without the two square sails, not only would her speed and power be hopelessly compromised, but her long, straight keel would hugely hamper her maneuverability.

He was her eager student. He learned that he could run up to anchor in Newport Harbor at night if the breeze had enough west in it, and he could get her anchor and leave Newport under sail, with the yawl boat in her davits, clearing Fort Adams and Castle Hill, if the morning wind was westerly or better still northwest. He and *Shenandoah* took advantage of what conditions offered and what *Shenandoah* gradually taught him she could do. He knew when conditions were right. Bound up the Mystic River for the Seaport Museum, he needed the wind in the southeast to keep from being blanketed by the buildings on the riverside; he would likely stow all sails but the topsail and topgallant and let the southeasterly carry her upriver, then stop her after the bridge by backing the topsails, get the yawl boat into the water, and push her to the Seaport dock. He knew the wind had to be west of southwest to carry sail through the jetties into Nantucket Harbor. He knew that when tacking she needed the topsails braced up sharp on the new tack at just the right moment to pull her through the maneuver, and he knew how much room and time the maneuver required. He learned that she had no weather helm, and no lee helm either, that her long, straight keel kept her on course, and that he could leave her to herself while he looked around and studied her. And he learned that the 20 tons of lead he had stuffed in her bilges when he got her home was not only required for ballast but needed to help her carry her way through a tack.

Home in Noank, Connecticut, on the Mystic River after a five-year circumnavigation with his family in a home-built replica of Joshua Slocum's *Spray*, Maynard remembers,

"It just so happened that that week *Shenandoah* came up the river with this Mariner Scout troop. They'd come up to spend the weekend at the Seaport. So, he came by, and being Bob, with his binoculars, he spotted my family's boat, modeled after Joshua Slocum's *Spray*. He knew right away what it was. He may have already known something about the boat, knowing him. The catalog in his brain is just so incredible. So somehow—I think they took the yawl boat—he got back down the river from the Seaport to check out our boat. I was a boat nut already. . . . So anyway, my dad said to Bob, 'Hey, I got this kid that would like to come sailing with you.' And Bob said, 'Sure. C'mon aboard. We got a week, and we'll go back to the Vineyard.'

"I was this little fifteen-year-old kid, and I jumped right in and started to learn about it—climbing around, crawling all over the topsails. And I'll never forget. We got underway. Scott Young was the mate. We sailed through Watch Hill passage and out into Rhode Island Sound with all sails set, going about nine knots with a fair wind . . . and Bob was out on the chains at the bow, watching the bow wave, which is very unusual for him, not to be at the helm, and the dog jumped overboard. Scotty Young was at the helm, and they had that boat hove-to and the yawl boat in the water, and they went and picked up that dog before any of us really knew what was going on. It was such a display of seamanship. And I was so impressed with that."

The dog in question may have been Black Dog, sometimes known as "the dog that started it all," or one of her many offspring. Douglas does not remember for sure. At any rate, Maynard became bosun and later mate on *Shenandoah*. He bought from Douglas a 45-foot Scottish Zulu fishing ketch named *Violet* and overhauled her for a sailing voyage to Tahiti with his own family; supervised a major rebuild of the Coastwise Packet Company's second schooner, the 92-foot *Alabama*; and did an extensive rebuild of Charlene Douglas's 50-foot cutter *McNab*. Maynard now lives on Martha's Vineyard, where he builds high-value houses for year-round and summer islanders.

It became a familiar story, a glimpse becoming a devotion. "My story starts a little while ago," Dominic Zachorne wrote in *Slop Chest* (2020), "in the summer of 1982 when we—Ma, Dad, my brother and I—were on our summer cruise on our 1929 English cutter *Ampelisca*. . . . This was the summer when my family met the Douglas family and secured a lasting friendship. . . . At anchor in Tarpaulin Cove enjoying the sun of the late day, Christian and I were playing on the housetop with Legos. . . . On this clear summer day Dad happened to notice, coming over the hill where the lighthouse stands, square sails, then headsails and a large head rig. It was like watching one of Ma's Horatio

Among Douglas's entrenched preoccupations is his encyclopedic catalog and history of every ancient, wooden, traditionally designed and built schooner he has heard of or come across, no matter its vintage, floating or not. He does not merely remember such craft. He will try relentlessly to persuade someone in his circle of crew, friends, and acquaintances to take on the forlorn schooner's remains and "put her right." Pictured here is the 70-foot *L. A. Jeffries*, a coasting schooner active for more than a century. When freights dried up for working sail, her owner removed her centerboard and installed a diesel engine in the middle of her main hold. Douglas persuaded one of his former *Shenandoah* mates to accept the challenge of her restoration, though his efforts were ultimately unavailing.

Hornblower movies. From around this headland came a ghost all in white from a time now gone by. It was cool!

"Captain Douglas invited us for dinner aboard *Shenandoah*, and we all boarded *Shenandoah*'s Whitehall and rowed back to the schooner. Robbie and Jamie, the captain's older boys, took me and Christian around the vessel. . . . We were on a tall ship, and it was huge, with blocks equal to our two heads put together and ropes as big as our arms. . . . After thirty-six years of knowing that schooner, it does not seem as massive as it did that first time I walked the deck, though she is no less impressive."

Zachorne was nine years old when he met Captain Douglas at Tarpaulin Cove. He, too, has been bosun and mate on *Shenandoah*. He spent a summer in command of

Sheeting *Shenandoah*'s inner jib requires a crowd. Tom Reynolds, the mate, is all the way forward. Next to him is Roger Hathaway, Alex Moravia, then Harry Dickerson, Matthew Stackpole, and Peter Crawford.

Alabama, and he has supervised the rigging and down-rigging of the schooner in the spring and fall. He operates Dominic Zachorne Ship Modeler in Wickford, Rhode Island, and is now hard at work at the reconstruction of *Raider*, a Bristol Channel pilot cutter Douglas bought during the visit to Ireland when he acquired the Zulu fishing ketch *Violet*. *Raider* has spent the years since her acquisition in the cool, dark Black Dog Tall Ships museum, colloquially known as the "cement building," just waiting, it seems, for Zachorne or someone to tackle the reconstruction job.

Matthew Stackpole was born on Nantucket. His father, Edouard A. Stackpole, was a journalist, marine historian, and curator of Mystic Seaport Museum from 1951 to 1966. A college sophomore, Matthew was working at Mystic Seaport for the summer of 1965 as an apprentice to master rigger Art Kimberly, later captain and owner of the brigantine *Romance,* when word came that *Shenandoah* was bound for the Seaport. "So, Toby Hall and I—Toby was a rigger that year too—got on the little Mystic Seaport tug called *Weir* and got aboard *Shenandoah* in Fishers Island Sound and then sailed in. And actually, there was a photograph in the *New London Day* of us coming through, the vessel coming through the bridge, and Toby and I were up on the topsail yard because we were used to climbing around boats, obviously. And that's how I first met Bob."

Stackpole got a job as a deckhand in the summer of 1966, "and that was my introduction. I'd never sailed on a big boat. My sailing experience had been on a catboat, crewing in the Mystic River. One time I got to sail to Nantucket on the *Yankee* with a guy who bought the boat from Irving Johnson, and on that trip I did sail; that was my one big-boat experience before coming to work on the schooner." In his second year aboard *Shenandoah*, Stackpole served as bosun; then he moved up to mate for the next three and a half years. In those early days, the mate shared the captain's cabin with

Douglas, so Stackpole's long tenure and lifelong friendship with Douglas and his family offers an acutely observed view of Douglas when his trials were behind him at last.

"I was thinking that I probably lived in the after cabin with Bob longer than anyone did," Stackpole recalled, "because I was there for three and a half years. George Adams would have been there for two and a half. And then of course Bob got married, so there was nobody else who got to do that. Bob's favorite book when he was young was *Jim Davis* by John Masefield. It's a story Masefield wrote about a young boy living on the Cornwall coast who becomes intrigued—stumbles across—smugglers. And they take him in, and he's with them in their adventures. It's a cave on the Cornwall coast where they keep a vessel that they go out and scavenge with. It's a marvelous story. I know it's one of the ones that influenced my dad. And it's interesting, because various people I've known over the years have said the same thing, that it's a magic book in some ways. But it's all about traveling and the people, the night riders. It's a cool story. Anyway, that's just the sort of thing that we'd talk about."

Stackpole's memory of their evening conversations and their shared enjoyment of Masefield's book suggests the story's certain grip on a young boy's imagination. But there was in Masefield's yarn a particular touchstone that must have made a permanent, albeit latent home for itself in young Robert Douglas's memory.

Marah Gorsuch, the smuggler who befriended Jim and his chum Hugh, watched them trying to sail a boat they had made from a most un-boat-like box. He was unimpressed by their design and their seamanship, so he led them to a cave that served as one of his hideouts and made them a gift from loot the smugglers had stolen from the Crown:

> 'Come in here,' he said, shoving us in front of him, 'and see what the Queen'll give you. Shut your eyes. That's the style. Now open.' When we opened our eyes we could hardly keep from shouting with pleasure. There on the ground, kept upright by a couple of bricks, was a three-foot model of a revenue cutter, under all her sail except the big square foresail which was neatly folded upon her yard. She was perfect aloft, even to her pennant; and on deck she was perfect too, with beautiful little model guns, all brass, on their carriages, pointing through the port holes.
> 'Oh!' we exclaimed. 'Oh! Is she really for us, for our very own?'
> 'Why, yes,' he said. 'At least she's for you, Mr. What's-your-name. Jim, I think you call yourself.'

Shenandoah anchored in Kettle Cove on the north shore of Naushon Island, waiting for a breeze.

When asked what led a Midwestern boy from flying jets to historic sailing vessels, Stackpole says, "I think it was his time on the Vineyard, sailing his Vineyard 15 and loving the water. That story about him swimming out to his 28-foot schooner *North Star* in one of the hurricanes battering the Vineyard to make sure she was okay, and his love for that. I don't know how he began to form, if you think of it really, his life's work in understanding ship design and American maritime history, both schooners and other vessels. I mean, his knowledge is just encyclopedic. And I don't know how that all happened. It happened over time. I do know that one time when I was on the schooner we went to

Mystic again, and it just turned out, coincidentally, that Howard Chapelle was giving a talk at Mystic. And we went to the talk, Bob and I, and we invited Howard to come see the boat. Bob was so excited because, as you know, *Shenandoah*'s design was based on a vessel that was in Howard's book.

"So, we took him down to the schooner—we almost had to take him hostage to get him there. We were on both sides, and he walked down. He got on the boat, had a walk around, never said a word, went ashore and walked away without saying a word. Bob was both mad and sad, I think. He really wanted to show this guy the vessel that Chapelle's book inspired. Chapelle just didn't seem to have any interest.

"Here was the real thing. Not something on a page. This was the real thing, with sails, you know. It was just frustrating. And Bob was annoyed by that. It's funny too, another time we were tied up where we always tied up there—just below where *Brilliant* ties up. And P.J. Matthews, who built the *Mystic Whaler*, came by. She was a schooner in the passenger trade, built after *Shenandoah* began operating in southern New England waters. Matthews, studying *Shenandoah* and especially her rig, said to Bob, 'You know, it looks great. She's so pretty, and all those great masts and those big sails. That rig, that's fantastic. But, you know, nobody will care. Do you know, it costs you more money to have enough crew to go up there in the rigging? We don't have any of that on the *Mystic Whaler*.'"

Matthews had not understood that the larger vessel, the more complicated rig, and young crew climbing in the rigging—"they called it a big jungle gym," Douglas says—were essential elements of Douglas's conception. Like Matthews, Chapelle did not appreciate what Douglas had done. He had made an inspiration real. *Joe Lane* was no longer merely a subject of Chapelle's research. She was now *Shenandoah*, in business and under sail.

Chapter Nine

Course Changes

CHARLENE LAPOINTE, PRETTY, dark-haired, vivacious, a whirlwind of a woman now in her seventies, grew up in the village of Padanaram in South Dartmouth, Massachusetts. She married Robert Douglas on May 22, 1970, the kickoff moment to a decade in Douglas's life defined by change and a quickening pace.

Charlene was born in 1942, and she had met Douglas during the winter of 1963 – 64 in South Bristol, Maine, at Harvey Gamage's shipyard. Actually, she had seen him briefly in 1960, aboard the three-masted passenger schooner *Victory Chimes,* where she was a deckhand and galley slave. Douglas's memory of that occasion is unclear. She was cleaning the heads and working in the fo'c's'le of the *Chimes* one day in 1960 when she was told by Frederick "Boyd" Guild, master of the *Chimes*, to bring coffee and cookies on deck for a visitor.

"So I went 'as is,' covered with soot, dust, and everything and gave them coffee and cookies. And that's when I first saw him," Charlene remembers. "I served them, but Boyd got a little pissed because I didn't clean up before coming on deck."

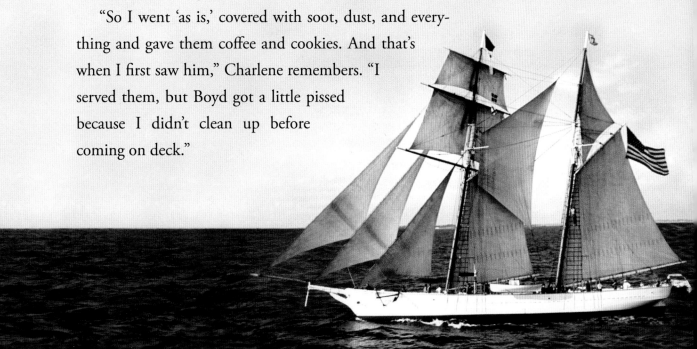

Remembering Charlene's later visit to South Bristol, Douglas admits to his wife, "When you came in the '63-'64 winter to Harvey's, I didn't know you'd been on board the *Chimes* back in 1960."

"You didn't know, no, and back in '60 I didn't have any idea who you were. I said to Boyd, 'Who was that man anyhow?' And Boyd said, 'Oh, he's nice enough. He's got more money than he needs, though.' And I remember that comment."

"Who would say a thing like that?" Douglas says. "Nice guy."

Douglas was generally welcomed into the Maine windjammer fraternity, largely because of his warm association with Havilah Hawkins, a widely acknowledged innovator and leader in the business. Still, Douglas's youth and inexperience, his enviable financial resources, and his determination to build for himself a vessel so vastly different from the venerable bald-headed fore-and-aft schooners then dominating the Down East passenger trade nourished a competitive skepticism. Douglas's plan to ply the same trade—but not to poach customers from their Down East territory—and his obviously fierce commitment to master a steep learning curve eventually mended the doubters' disgruntlement over the Midwesterner.

Douglas explains comments like the one Boyd Guild made in the narrow marine terms that make sense to him: "Well, I made them feel bad. Let's face it, nobody down there ever had a topmast. See? There was no such thing as a topmast in the Maine windjammer fleet until I came along. And they didn't—'What's a yard?' they would say. Something in the back of the house that you grow tomatoes in. So, obviously they didn't like that. Eventually, finally, everybody had topmasts."

As time passed and Douglas piled up successful years in the business in his southern New England neighborhood, he and his Maine windjammer counterparts became mutually admiring friends.

Shenandoah's 1972 season closed with rain and fog. A couple of dry days before unbending the canvas sails were a must, so Douglas planned a friends-and-crew cruise, extending invitations to several Maine captains and their families. All ages were welcomed. One long day would be required to undress the schooner, and a surplus of hands would help the work go quickly. Most of Douglas's summer crew had vanished, bound for school.

A first-person account of that postseason sail by this writer appeared in the February 1972 edition of *Soundings* magazine. "With less than a day's notice there assembled in Vineyard Haven . . . Captain Havilah 'Buds' Hawkins of the schooner *Mary Day*, his wife and son Havilah; also Captain Orville Young of the schooner *Stephen Taber*, with his wife, son, and mate; and Captain Mike Young of the *Mattie*."

Twenty hands, young and old, men and women, signed on—just enough to hoist the main- and foresail. *Shenandoah* made stops in Newport and twice in Tarpaulin Cove. Some of the guests brought musical instruments. "Evening meals aboard the schooner were long-lasting affairs. The talk of boats went on and on beneath the swinging kerosene lamps, and long after the gimballed saloon tables had been cleared, the names of famous vessels and the men who ran them rose to the gentle light. As if by magic, the trappings of the modern world slipped away and were forgotten; and we breathed deeply the air of past years when sails and schooners and solitary anchorages were the privileges of seamen on this coast."

Charlene was an experienced sailor herself, mainly on Mariner Scout summer cruises on the brigantine *Yankee* out of the Outdoorsman in Fairhaven, Massachusetts, and on *Tabor Boy*, the school ship of Tabor Academy in Marion, Massachusetts, but also on the *Victory Chimes* and the charter yacht *C'est La Vie*. When Douglas was crewing for Havilah Hawkins out of Camden, she was sailing aboard the *Chimes* along with William Bunting, who became bosun on *Shenandoah* during her first summer under sail in 1964. She is very proud that she, along with Douglas and their four boys, all have 100-ton master's licenses.

Captain and Mrs. Robert S. Douglas aboard *Shenandoah* at Boothbay Harbor, Maine, at the end of September 1976.

The courtship between the schooner captain and the Mariner Scout was conducted over a decade in anchorages up and down the New England coast, aboard *Shenandoah* during summer weeks when the schooner hosted sailing trips for the Mariner Scout troop from Padanaram, and, as time passed, often in the kitchen of Charlene's mother's house when Douglas could find the right occasion, given wind and weather and day of the week, to anchor for a night in Padanaram. Charlene's mother, Gertrude, was a gifted cook, and Douglas was doubly rewarded for each visit.

"He would sail in and out of Padanaram all the time," Charlene says.

"Occasionally," says Douglas.

"Oh, he came and went with great regularity," Charlene counters. "I would see him coming through Quicks Hole. On a clear day from the yacht club, I could see him coming."

"At least the topsails," Douglas interjects, trying to at least keep the log of this courtship straight.

She was teaching sailing for the Mariner Scouts at the New Bedford Yacht Club, whose home base is in Padanaram. "I would run home, wash my hair, sit under the hair dryer. And then I would run back to the club and pretend I'd been there the whole time. And, in the meantime, I would always have a crust made, so I could make his lemon meringue pie, which is his favorite."

Charlene had inherited her mother's culinary savvy, and she had developed an understanding of how useful it could be in certain pursuits.

In the winter of 1963 – 64, Charlene, "escorted by Bill Bunting," as Bob remembers it, spent a night in a house Elaine Jenson and her husband, proprietors of the Coveside Inn, had available, one that could be heated. *Shenandoah*'s construction had begun, and Douglas was in South Bristol observing, overseeing, and joining in the work. During the visit, Bunting and Douglas studied for their Coast Guard master's licenses. Charlene's job was to ask the test questions.

At 17, Bunting, a sailing buddy from *Victory Chimes* days, had told Charlene about Douglas and the boat he was building and suggested the trip to South Bristol. "Billy wrote me a letter and said, 'I'm going to be bo'sun on this new vessel.' And he drew me a picture of *Shenandoah*. He said, 'C'mon, let's go up and see him.'

Before joining Douglas on *Shenandoah*, Bunting had sailed with Captain Christopher Sheldon on *Albatross* as one of the student crew, and he was fortunate to be one of the survivors when she sank in the Gulf of Mexico in 1961. After his season on *Shenandoah*, Bunting sailed again with Sheldon, this time as chief mate on Sheldon's 130-foot *Verona*. Bunting was no longer a member of her crew when, on her second voyage under Sheldon in 1965, *Verona* caught fire and sank near the island of Bioko in the Bight of Benin, off Cameroon on the west coast of Africa. All hands escaped. Bunting turned later to farming and writing. He is the author of highly regarded histories, including *Sea Struck* and *Maine on Glass*.

Charlene's second encounter with her future husband made a more detailed impression than the first. "I saw this man, big man, black-and-red-checked woolen shirt. It was like, good luck, he doesn't say a word. He doesn't say anything. He just comes along. He doesn't say anything. And, I'm a lot of fun. And he was going up the stairs into what was his office. He had a little office space to do his own business. And this German shepherd was on the stairway, and Robert went up, patted the dog a little bit. Her name was Lady.

"He stopped and played with the dog, like he does. And I said to myself, 'He's okay. Maybe he's okay. You know?' And I saw him again that night when they were studying for their license exams. And I thought, 'Well, he does talk. And he's smart.' It was fun. Then I spent the night there, and I drove home with Billy in my new Karmann Ghia, which was a little Italian car. I had my license."

After their wedding, for some reason no one can explain, the determination to build a restaurant rose to the top of the newlyweds' agenda. Vineyard Haven, the waterfront village historically known as Holme's Hole, is part of the town of Tisbury. In the late nineteenth and early twentieth centuries, it was a busy stop for coastwise schooners under sail on easterly or westerly courses, lugging miscellaneous freights. In 1970, the year-round population of Dukes County, which comprises the six towns of Martha's Vineyard island plus the Elizabeth Islands town of Gosnold, was about 7,000 souls. Restaurants were scarce, especially in Vineyard Haven. There was the Artcliff Diner, serving a plain, hearty menu appreciated by its loyal patrons, or you could get something to eat at the bowling alley next to the Artcliff. Douglas and his bride breakfasted at the Artcliff, across Beach Road from the Coastwise Packet Company dock. The diner was a go-to, reliable stop for islanders and had been for years. It flourishes today despite sporting the very same, very plain look it had fifty years ago, though the cuisine has become more artful and alluring.

"I spent the weekend with Bob, but I had to go back to college," Charlene recalls, "and the only place you could get breakfast was the Artcliff. They had Mother Parker doughnuts. And he said, 'This is what we're going to do. We're going to build a restaurant,' and he drew a picture of the Black Dog on a napkin."

Douglas already had the yellow pine timbers from a razed power plant in Salem, Massachusetts. They were an unplanned acquisition, having arrived with a 9,000-pound, nine-inch muzzle-loading Dahlgren cannon, vintage 1855, that had been part of the armament of the steam frigate *Wabash*. "I don't remember the exact time frame," he says, "but I bought the cannon from a friend who knew I was foolish. He called me up to tell me it was in a junkyard in Blue Hill, Massachusetts, south of Boston. 'Would you like it?' he wanted to know. I didn't know exactly what it was, but he described it, and I said, 'Yes, but you have to get it down here.' So, one day somebody drives a big semi-tractor

The big yellow pine timbers of the Black Dog Tavern came to Douglas in a package deal with this 9,000-pound cannon that now rests outside the tavern door, pointing out to sea.

dump trailer into the driveway, and it's full of hard pine and the cannon. And the guy makes a deal for the cannon if I also take the hard pine. I remember some computations, as if I was buying firewood. It was all big stock, like 10 x 12 timbers. So that showed up with the gun, and it all stayed on the ground. Maybe I put the gun someplace else, but the wood all stayed in the pile. It must have been there a couple of years. And there was just enough for the restaurant."

The size and shape of the Black Dog Tavern were dictated by the dimensions of those timbers, and it was named for Douglas's own dog, a compact female black Labrador with four white feet, but also of course after the eight-fingered character in *Treasure Island*.

On the beach, sitting where the Black Dog is now, next to the Coastwise dock, there was a building—an aged, weathered boathouse of the most primitive sort, first named Ocmulgee after a Vineyard-owned whaleship, but later known as Hickory Hall—whose sign is now displayed in the restaurant. It is a remarkable if inconsequential coincidence that the whaleship *Ocmulgee*, Captain Abraham Osborn Jr., was owned by the Osborn family of Edgartown. She had formerly sailed from Vineyard Haven, where the boat-house that the Black Dog Tavern replaced stood. In 1862, hunting whales near the

Azores, she was captured, burned, and sunk by the Confederate raider *Alabama*, Captain Raphael Semmes, who, as a United States Navy officer before the war, had been a frequent dinner guest of the Osborns at their house in Edgartown. When the war began, Captain Semmes transferred his allegiance to the Confederacy.

"My brothers and I had always talked about what a wonderful spot Hickory Hall would be for a restaurant," Douglas says. "And you could build a restaurant pretty easily back then. There were no zoning rules until later in the 1970s. All you needed was permission for a cesspool. After zoning came along, you couldn't keep horses on the waterfront in front of my house, you couldn't do a lot of things. I'm sure you couldn't have built a restaurant on the beach."

Douglas drew sketches of what it would look like for his friend Allan Miller, a builder who had worked with Douglas's brother David, an architect, and who possessed an aesthetic in perfect harmony with Douglas's own. Miller hand-planed the pine planking for the dining room floor and the raised panels over the huge fireplace. He built the restaurant's giant fireplace too. He not only constructed the restaurant but was its first manager and cook. Miller had a casual, lively, inviting, unbusinesslike way about him, and that became the Tavern's way. It was profitable every year he ran it.

As built, the original restaurant had limited capacity. A porch ran along the waterside and the entrance to the building. The kitchen was open to the dining room, and there was a counter and stools so a customer could chat with the chef while eating breakfast. Before long a large, hugely appealing, languorous nude, commissioned by Miller and painted by highly regarded Vineyard painter Stanley Murphy, graced the kitchen. There was no conventional heating system. Miller's fireplace was at the north end of the dining room, and a big railroad cast iron woodstove was at the other end. When well fed, the two heat sources in combination could keep the dining room warm but not hot, especially when a northeast storm beat against the dining room's harbor-facing French doors, driving the surf itself up to within a few feet of the building. The fireplace sometimes did not draw well because its flue was competing for air with the big exhaust fans in the kitchen, and diners' eyes might water as they left the restaurant. Flooding was not an issue, because the building sat above the beach sand on treated piers like those used to build docks. There was no cellar. Anyone with a hammer and a casual acquaintance with the application of cedar shingles to walls and gambrel roofs joined in the effort to enclose the building and later became a devoted customer. The music was a steady diet of

The Black Dog Tavern entryway (top) and interior (above). Massive pine timbers establish the seagoing flavor.

James Taylor, Linda Ronstadt, and Carole King, with a bit of Tammy Wynette expertly chosen for time and circumstance.

"Well, to begin with, everybody did everything. All your friends were on the building and shingling crew, waitressing, baking, and everything else," is Douglas's description of the unusual enterprise. He said a waterfront town like Vineyard Haven, his adopted home, ought to have a restaurant where sailors could get good chowder and tell tales. "I tell my friends, 'Don't move to a town that doesn't have a good restaurant in it, because then you have to become a restaurateur.'" Construction began on July 13, 1970, when Miller had Douglas drive in the stakes that marked the building's location. The Black Dog opened for business on January 1, 1971.

The all-are-welcome approach to the hospitality business included contributions from friends with allied talents. For example, Sally Knight, wife of Lambert Knight—formerly captain of the Woods Hole Oceanographic Institution's 143-foot steel ketch *Atlantis,* built by Burmeister and Wain in Copenhagen, Denmark in 1930—made wonderful clam chowder, soups, and pies and sometimes managed the cash register. She delivered the goods to the restaurant in her green MG sports car with the big chowder pot in the passenger seat and the top down. Charlene Douglas made desserts, and artistic staff members and friends designed T-shirts for workers, then for sale to the public. The design featuring Black Dog herself caught on quickly, and before long there was a catalog, then a retail outlet, a bakery, a second restaurant, and Black Dog stores elsewhere in island and mainland towns along the East Coast.

Douglas has no persuasive explanation for the feverish 1970s. "First of all, to get married, build a tugboat, and build a restaurant all in the same year, obviously I was bored or something. One of those things would have been enough to keep anyone busy," he says. But perhaps exuberance is a better explanation. It was a spectacularly happy time for Douglas. The Coast Guard struggles were history, or at least were not urgent at the moment, *Shenandoah* was performing as he had imagined she would, and her passengers loved the experience. Business flourished. There was no obvious need, beyond a desire on Douglas's part for good food in a congenial atmosphere, to get into the restaurant business.

Unfortunately, an error in siting the restaurant building placed it inches over the boundary between Douglas's land and the Tilton Lumber Company property next door. The president of the big bank in town was acquiring the lumber yard along with the historic Seaman's Bethel property, farther north along the shore, to sell to the Steamship

Authority, which had an eye on expansion. Douglas had never enjoyed an untroubled relationship with the ferry company, mainly because he criticized it for making too many trips to the island bringing too many people, which, he forecasted, would certainly ruin Martha's Vineyard. Not surprisingly, the wily bank president ultimately had his way, and Douglas would have had to straighten out the matter of the Black Dog's modest encroachment on what had become Steamship Authority land except that both sides decided to leave well enough alone. The ferry company made the former lumber company land into a parking lot and staging area for automobiles.

Chapter Ten

Why Not a Tugboat?

DOUGLAS COULD LOOK OUT from the Black Dog Tavern in 1971 and see not just one but two of his schooners swinging to their moorings. His fascination with what he, and sometimes only he, could distinguish in a well-designed vessel, no matter how old, battered, or forlorn, had led him in 1967 to the pilot schooner *Alabama*. Perhaps he was prescient, or perhaps the Thomas F. McManus – designed, fully powered fishing schooner just caught his eye. McManus's designs were celebrated for their sea-keeping, endurance, speed, and ability to jog along with a small crew while the fisher-men were off in their dories after cod—think Spencer Tracy in the 1937 film *Captains Courageous*. Douglas had no plan for the boat, but he bought her anyway.

Built in 1926 for the Mobile Bar Pilots Association, *Alabama* had spent her life stationed at the entrance to Mobile Bay to accommodate pilots awaiting ships enter-ing or departing the bay. Retired from service in 1966, her schooner hull had never been rigged for sail. When built, she had been fitted with a short riding sail rig.

She needed substantial reconstruction. Lacking an identified use, she lay on her mooring next to *Shenandoah* in Vineyard Haven Harbor for nearly thirty years. By 1994, when the market for week-long cruises for adults was weakening while interest in sailing adventures for grammar school children from Martha's Vineyard and elsewhere in the Northeast was growing, that trend coincided with the availability and interest of former *Shenandoah* mate Gary Maynard in taking charge of the needed rebuild. Maynard replaced nearly 90 percent of the original vessel, and Douglas designed and installed a schooner rig with two gaff topsails.

The schooner *Alabama* was designed by Thomas F. McManus, whose Gloucester fishing schooner designs were admired by many, including Bob Douglas. Built in 1926, the *Alabama* lived her first life as a floating dormitory for the pilots of the Mobile Bar Pilots Association, who guided ships into and out of Mobile. Retired in 1966, she was put up for sale, and Douglas bought her. She had never been rigged as an outright sailing vessel, though she did have a steadying rig—not shown in this photograph—and a small wheelhouse all the way aft. She was powered by twin diesel engines. She lay on her mooring in Vineyard Haven Harbor for nearly 30 years before Douglas rebuilt her and put her in service carrying schoolchildren.

Alabama went back into service in 1998, this time under sail, conducting children's cruises, daysails, weddings, celebrations of all sorts, and even funerals. Indeed, Douglas's friend Bernie Holzer was memorialized aboard *Alabama* and saluted by a passing Steamship Authority ferry on which he had worked for decades.

Alabama's three-decade hiatus stood in stark contrast to the speed with which Douglas had created *Shenandoah*; in *Alabama*'s case, the satisfaction of mere possession had apparently sustained the dream until the missing pieces fell into place and she became the second Black Dog Tall Ship.

A new family and a new restaurant did not extinguish Douglas's unquenchable enthusiasm for additions to his fleet. The targets need not be wooden, schooners, historic, or old.

Alabama at anchor in Mobile Bay during her first incarnation, her short riding rig furled.

The surprise was that on the flimsiest of pretexts, Douglas decided to design and build a tugboat. Among the various and numberless boats that have passed through his hands, *Whitefoot,* the businesslike, twin-engine, 65-foot tugboat built at Halter Marine in Louisiana, was only the second vessel designed and built to his exacting requirements. *Whitefoot* became the chief asset of Whitefoot Towing and Salvage Company, which Douglas created in 1970, at the beginning of the decade of such significant change in the schooner captain's business and personal life. But, why a tugboat?

He had use for a tugboat for predictable occasions—such as shifting engine-less *Shenandoah* to the shipyard in Fairhaven each spring to be hauled and painted, then returning her to her Vineyard Haven mooring—and for those that were unpredictable, such as finding himself becalmed at the west end of Vineyard Sound with the current about to change against him and miles to go to reach Tarpaulin Cove on a Friday night. Tarpaulin met several of Douglas's narrowly curated criteria for anchorages he adored. For practical reasons, he needed to be within an easy sail or push to Vineyard Haven on a Saturday morning in order to disembark his passengers at Saturday midday. Tarpaulin fit the bill. But that is a mere prosaic necessity. Aesthetically, Douglas loved Tarpaulin Cove, and he loved both the thought and the sight of *Shenandoah* anchored there. The cove was a home away from home for him and his schooner.

On occasion, when Tarpaulin was within reach but essentially unreachable because of wind, weather, and current, he could call upon the *James J. Minot*, the 50-foot work-boat he had traded for from his brother David. Sometimes Douglas would run the *Minot* while *Shenandoah*'s mate steered the schooner; other times a former *Shenandoah* mate such as Scott Young or Bill Mabie, who had become professional mariners and settled on the Vineyard, could be called on short notice to do the job using *Minot*. Ralph Packer, who owns the fuel business R.M. Packer Company and its allied Packer Marine in Vineyard Haven, was another friend who could be pressed into service. Packer Marine moved R.M. Packer fuel products to Nantucket and the Elizabeth Islands and took on other towing jobs for outside customers. When called upon, Packer could fire up *Minot* or one of his own tugs—the small but mighty 28-foot *Ursa* and the slightly larger *Vega*—and assist as needed.

After retiring from fishing his 60-foot Eastern-rigged dragger *Roann,* which he had built in 1947 and sold thirteen years later, Roy W. Campbell, a Vineyard Haven resident, earned his living as a bay scalloper and tugboat captain. (Owned and rebuilt by Mystic Seaport Museum at a cost of $1.2 million, *Roann* is now a traveling museum exhibit.) Campbell ran the Packer tugs and had once rescued *Shenandoah* off the beach at the head of Vineyard Haven Harbor after she was driven ashore by a furious northeaster. As the gale screeched, Campbell hauled *Shenandoah* into deep water and shifted her safely over to the south side of the Steamship Authority dock across the harbor. It was a remarkable demonstration of seamanship by an extremely clever boat handler in the tiny *Ursa*. Campbell was another mariner whom Douglas called on occasionally for an assist from *Ursa* or *Minot*. And Douglas, in turn, made the occasional tow with *Minot*, acting as Campbell's mate. "Roy had been very useful to me," Douglas says.

Douglas recalls acting as Campbell's mate aboard *Minot* to tow a Packer fuel barge to Nantucket when Packer's own tugs were otherwise occupied. "It was very foggy. We delivered the barge and had a bite to eat in Nantucket before the return trip. You couldn't see the harbor entrance from the town, but we were hauling the barge home anyway.

Easterly gales harry Vineyard Haven Harbor mercilessly. Here, left to right, Robert Soros's *Juno*, designed by Nat Benjamin and built by Gannon and Benjamin in Vineyard Haven, *Alabama*, and *Shenandoah* ride out the worst of a screecher. The madcap adventurer in the foreground is unidentified.

"I remember it was thick fog and just rough enough with a light northerly wind and a westerly current meeting a northerly current at the end of the Nantucket jetties to get *Minot* jumping up and down. *Minot* had no radar or GPS, and only an ancient single sideband radio for communication. 'How are you going to find the Tuckernuck buoy?' I said to Roy. 'This is crazy.'

"Roy said, 'We'll just keep the wind on this side of my nose,'" Douglas recalls, imitating Campbell's nose tap. "I'll never forget it. So, he keeps an eye on his watch—of course, he had made that run more than a couple of times—and eventually we come alongside the Tuckernuck buoy. He shuts the engine off. 'Hear it?' he says. 'Ding, ding, ding.' And he starts her up again, and we took off for the Cross Rip buoy, and he did that almost all the way home."

Ursa was primitive, with no accommodations to speak of and no heat, and the jobs Campbell did year-round with his regular mate, his neighbor Charlie Conroy, were tricky, often in difficult weather. The 28-footer had no surplus of power or size. Douglas admired Campbell's skill, experience, and toughness. Perhaps he was swayed by the prospect of having a proper tug at hand when he needed one; perhaps he just thought that Campbell deserved a bigger, better, purpose-built vessel for towing and salvage work; or perhaps he was drawn to the prospect of designing and building another boat. Douglas has no answer, except to suggest that all three motivations contributed.

Douglas and Campbell discussed the possibility, but there was no carefully detailed business plan forecasting meaningful financial success. Campbell told Douglas, "If you build it, I'll find the business." Which he did, although not enough and not consistently.

Charlene Douglas says, "We built *Whitefoot* for Roy, or at least we wouldn't have built it if it weren't for Roy."

Douglas got in touch with Halter Marine in Lockport, Louisiana, whose in-house architect, Sal Guarino, and Douglas worked out a design for what turned out to be something other than a common tugboat. *Whitefoot* more nearly resembled one of the oil rig supply boats that Halter Marine typically built—200- to 250-foot-long vessels with their pilothouse and accommodations forward and a long, open deck space for pipe and drilling-mud tankage aft. *Whitefoot* was shorter, but with her superstructure forward and a long, broad deck space aft, where a crane was eventually mounted, causing *Whitefoot*'s compass to spin erratically. Still, *Whitefoot* had a wide range of useful attributes. Powered by twin 250-horsepower diesels, she could do more than tow, and Douglas was especially pleased with her versatility. She cost $160,000.

Business-wise, she had good times and lean. Over thirteen years she worked for the US Navy, the Woods Hole Oceanographic Institute, the Coast Guard, the Marine Fisheries Service, the US Geologic Service, and several other clients. Campbell, in his mid-seventies when the tug went into service, was still sharp and sharp-edged. Caught in a storm offshore in *Whitefoot* while tending to Navy submarines on maneuvers, he would shut down the tug's engines, lie ahull, and eat nothing but peanut butter and ice cream until the gale swept by, a practice that did nothing to comfort the nerves or the digestion of the Navy personnel aboard the tug. Most notoriously, *Whitefoot* served as mother ship, restaurant, base, and towboat for the mechanized shark built for Stephen Spielberg and his crew during the filming of *Jaws*, the movie based on Nantucketer Peter Benchley's novel. The film production—or at least the lucrative early-spring, pre-tourist-season economic boost it gave islanders—is remembered fondly on the Vineyard.

This circa 1958 image, photographer unknown, is of interest for several reasons. First, this is the old Steamship Authority wharf in Vineyard Haven. The big shed sheltered freight arriving on dollies rather than in trailer trucks. Islanders could enter the shed and search for their deliveries or leave goods bound for the mainland, also kept there on dollies. At far left is the *Madison Edwards*, the Seaman's Bethel launch named for the chaplain who served mariners from the Cove House at Tarpaulin Cove, Naushon Island, across Vineyard Sound. When this photograph was taken, Austin Tower had replaced Edwards as bethel chaplain, and the Vineyard Haven Seaman's Bethel had taken on the work of the Cove House. Also in view is the double-ended ferry *Islander*, launched from the Maryland Drydock Company of Baltimore in 1950 and retired in 2007; she was a durable, reliable workhorse and consequently a great favorite of islanders. Finally, the *Irene May*, seen here alongside the freight shed, had been in mine-sweeping service during World War II. Douglas saw her in the summer of 1958 and liked her looks. He bought her in 1967, not as trim and well cared for as seen here, for use as a towboat and tender for *Shenandoah*, but she was not handy for the work, and he kept her only briefly.

Captain Campbell and *Whitefoot* managed to reignite the always simmering discontent between Douglas and the Woods Hole, Martha's Vineyard and Nantucket Steamship Authority. The Authority thought Douglas's two sailing vessels were in the way of its ferries entering and leaving Vineyard Haven. Douglas thought the ferries and the growing number of trips they made in and out of the harbor endangered his vessels and were taking up too much space in the mooring field. In addition, Douglas regarded the ferry line as the culprit responsible for the island's booming real estate development and for the growth of its year-round and seasonal populations. But then in September 1971, the steamer *Nobska*, 210 feet, built in 1925, the oldest vessel in the Steamship Authority's fleet, got herself aground in a thick fog. The steamer's master, Captain Pat Prudencio, drove her straight onto the beach sand about 75 yards south of the steamship wharf in Oak Bluffs. Captain Prudencio was so far south of the wharf where he ought to have docked that islanders suggested he was bound right up to town with her for a bite to eat.

That morning *Whitefoot* was underway in dungeon fog for Nantucket to collect a tow, this writer along as deckhand. *Whitefoot* altered course for Oak Bluffs when Captain Campbell heard of the grounding, arrived before any other assistance, put a hawser on *Nobska*'s stern, and began to pull. A favorite comment of the crusty Campbell was, "Don't worry, old son, when I put my hawser on her, she'll come right along," but this time the hawser parted. The tide was at about half ebb, and the situation was worsening. *Whitefoot* connected again with another hawser, and a Coast Guard vessel that had arrived to assist put a second hawser aboard the stricken ferry. This time, with all its passengers, freight, and automobiles still aboard, *Nobska* came free. The Steamship Authority bitterly disputed *Whitefoot*'s bill for the assistance, which did nothing to abate the durable hostility between Douglas and the ferry line. *Nobska* was retired from service in 1973. The last of the Atlantic seaboard's coastal steamers, she was scrapped in June 2006, despite strenuous efforts to raise funds to save her.

Hostilities flared again a year or so later when Captain Prudencio concluded his long service to the Steamship Authority by running another ferry, the revered double-ender *Islander,* into the starboard bow of *Shenandoah* on another thick-fog morning. *Shenandoah*, decommissioned for the winter, was lying on her mooring in Vineyard Haven at the time. Douglas demanded that the Steamship Authority's insurance pay for the considerable damage to his schooner and repay to him the deductible on Coastwise's insurance policy, which, after considerable debate, the ferry line did.

Whitefoot, always looked after devotedly by Captain Campbell, was sold in 1983 for $300,000. Campbell died in 2003.

Chapter 11

Coast Guard Redux

DOUGLAS HAD ALWAYS UNDERSTOOD that *Shenandoah* was massively overbuilt, being in some parts—the stern circle, for example—nearly solid wood. He also knew that the red oak from Harvey Gamage's woodlots was the same material that went into the construction of some two hundred remarkably durable offshore fishing vessels, little different in their fundamental construction from *Shenandoah,* that Gamage had built over the years, just like the dragger *Jane and Ursula,* which was built alongside *Shenandoah* in Gamage's shed and also launched in 1964.

As Gamage explained in an August 2, 1963, letter to the Coast Guard hearing that would decide whether *Shenandoah* should be allowed to operate with paying passengers, "For the past twenty odd years we have specialized in the construction of heavy wooden vessels." These had included minesweepers for the Navy during World War II. "The keel construction," he continued, "as well as the overall construction of Mr. Douglas's schooner, is heavier than that normally used in the construction of wooden fishing vessels of comparable size.

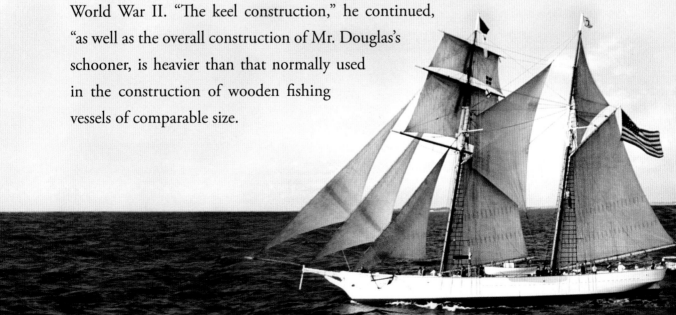

"During our many years of building heavy wooden fishing vessels for use in the New England fleet . . . our vessels . . . have [operated] without indications of structural weakness, and with the even heavier structural build-up of Mr. Douglas's vessel, it is the writer's considered opinion that the ruggedness built into this vessel will far exceed the requirements of any possible operating conditions that this vessel can encounter."

The significant difference between Gamage's offshore draggers and Douglas's "extreme clipper schooner," a difference whose implications Douglas did not completely appreciate when he reserved space in Gamage's building shed for *Shenandoah*'s construction, was that the fishing vessels operated year-round, constantly immersed and deluged in torrents of seawater. *Shenandoah,* in contrast, operated for three summer months each year and lived rain-washed on her Vineyard Haven mooring the rest of the time. If red oak was going to give itself up to rot, the conditions in which *Shenandoah* lived her life were very favorable for it.

Douglas knew that some of the longest-lived schooners operating in the Maine windjammer fleet had been built in Long Island, Connecticut, Maryland, the Chesapeake, and the Carolinas at the end of the nineteenth century, and he came to understand that the most ancient among them had migrated to Maine when the freight business for sailing vessels dried up to the south, not because they were falling apart from rotted red oak.

"Red oak planking, readily available in Maine, was not a good idea," Douglas wrote in 2014, as he began and shortly abandoned a kind of memoir, the "story of my *Shenandoah*." It was a story he unfurled in the plainest terms—detailing the choice of wood, fastenings, long scarfs, fair lines, and the name of every craftsman who contributed. Red oak, he said, was "fine for a fishing boat that is literally soaking in salt water most of her life. A laid-up vessel gets very little salt water touching her topside and waist, but lots of fresh water. Long-leaf yellow pine, white oak, or cypress would have lasted much longer." But there was little white oak timber to be had in Maine, and no hard pine or exotic hardwoods. Maine builders used what was at hand.

From 1965 to 2011, while *Shenandoah* and Douglas spent their summers carrying adult passengers and, later, grammar-school children on week-long excursions along the New England coast, each spring the vessel was subject to a safety inspection and recertification by the Coast Guard. Annual maintenance was sufficient to convince the Coast Guard inspectors of the schooner's seaworthiness, but the red oak with which *Shenandoah* was framed and planked was slowly succumbing to its natural vices.

For years the Coast Guard had regularly found some rot here and there but allowed Douglas to dig out the soft spots and replace the rot with what Douglas called "blow-out cement," a commercial body filler called Bondo. The planks were, after all, three inches thick. In the spring of 2007, however, the Coast Guard ordered that the vessel undergo a refastening program to check for defects in the existing fasteners and to repair and replace them as necessary. In response, the hull planking below the waterline was refastened on 25 percent of the frames at D.N. Kelly's Shipyard in Fairhaven. The Coast Guard also required the replacement of some topside planks that contained polyester resin filler in areas of previous rot.

In November of that year, still not satisfied, the Coast Guard demanded further work, including refastening the 75 percent of the planks that hadn't been refastened in the spring. The Coast Guard also wanted Douglas to replace eighteen topside planks because of rot.

Douglas contracted the Boothbay Harbor Shipyard for the work. No contract price was set, but he paid $700,000 when he left the yard, expecting further payments of $50,000 annually at six percent interest to begin one year after the work was satisfactorily completed. In the course of the work, rot was found elsewhere in oak stanchions and particularly in the round stern of the vessel, which was repaired entirely with white oak, generally regarded as a longer-lived material. Douglas returned *Shenandoah* to Vineyard Haven in the spring to begin her forty-fourth operating season, expecting to pay an additional $200,000 pursuant to a note issued by the yard.

Back at work in June, however, *Shenandoah* "began to leak a significant amount of water," according to court documents. She went back to Kelly's Shipyard, where the leak was investigated and corrected, but after being returned to service, the leaking recurred. After the sailing season she was returned to Kelly's for more investigation and work.

Ultimately, more than $221,000 of Boothbay's charges were deducted following the court's judgment that detailed, "among other things, missing bungs, empty fastener holes, improperly installed fasteners, use of an improper sealant, overly wide caulking seams, poorly installed caulking, and too-short futtock overlaps."

Boothbay Shipyard "admitted liability for its defective work and therefore for breach of contract and breach of warranty." In its unsuccessful appeal of the judge's order, the shipyard's lawyers claimed that "the court's judgment, if it is upheld, has rendered BYSY insolvent." They proposed a $65,000 settlement, which was rejected. A calculation by Douglas's lawyers detailed total costs to Boothbay at $518,000, not including $350,000 in legal fees. The court found that Kelly's Shipyard "repaired Boothbay's defective work and also conducted repairs that were beyond the scope of the contract between Coastwise (Douglas) and Boothbay."

Sturdy, shapely, carefully managed and sailed, *Shenandoah* and Douglas kept ahead of the Coast Guard's detailed annual assessments for forty-six years, doing what was necessary to keep the vessel in operating shape. But a new hurdle arose in 2011. In response to government estimates that Americans had gotten heavier over time, the Coast Guard required that the stability of licensed passenger vessels be recalculated assuming that each human cavorting on deck weighed 185 pounds instead of 165. The re-examination was especially important because passengers are mobile and likely to be on deck when the vessel is underway, rather than tucked away deep in the bilges like so many lead ballast ingots. Mobile weight on deck can have an especially meaningful and variable effect on stability.

In 2011, naval architect Christofer Melo of Padanaram conducted a stability experiment for *Shenandoah* at Kelly's Shipyard, using weighted barrels moved to selected stations on the schooner's deck with a crane. "*Shenandoah* went into service, and the rules for sailing vessels, for passenger sailing vessels, were largely written in response to her," Melo explained in 2020. "She was a first in this industry, as far as a new build, an engineless topsail schooner, and the Coast Guard realized that they didn't really have rules that covered this type of vessel, and much of what we have now for sailing vessel rules were written following her going into service. I told Captain Bob that day that it was probably the most nervous day I've ever had in thirty years in the business, because I didn't want to be the one to tell him that the vessel could no longer operate, after seeing her my entire life as a local icon.

"What the Coast Guard said was, since the vessel predated the existing sailing vessel rules, to have her analyzed by those rules would, in a way, be unfair, particularly since Captain Bob had not changed her. If you change your vessel, just like a building on land, you're bound by all the new rules that have come into play since the last time it was certified. But if you haven't changed it, generally it's considered, and the Coast Guard is understanding of this, that it's through no fault of yours that the rules are now different. So, what they said was, if you match the principal characteristics that the vessel displayed in her last incline test, the one that was done in Vineyard Haven [in 1964]—in other words, the weight, the longitudinal center of gravity, and particularly the vertical center of gravity—we won't force you to conform to the new sailing vessel rules. So, it gave us the opportunity to prove—as Captain Douglas had contended from the beginning—that the vessel had not been adversely changed throughout her entire life span.

"Vessels almost always change over fifty years, and those changes almost always impact their stability. So, I don't think the Coast Guard believed we could actually prove that Captain Douglas's memory was one hundred percent correct and that *Shenandoah* hadn't changed. So there again, adding to the tension and drama of that day in Fairhaven, we were essentially setting out to prove that fifty years of his recollections could be verified by this highly accurate procedure we were doing. Our goal that day was to show that the vessel had not gained in weight, that she had the same location placements in weight, and that her vertical center of gravity was no higher than it had been fifty years prior. That was the question that we set about to experimentally determine."

Douglas was certain that *Shenandoah*'s center of gravity was lower than it had been when she was first put in service, largely because of the work done on her in 2007 – 08, when half of her stanchions [which frame the bulwarks above her deck], weighing a total of three tons, had been removed from their deck-level locations.

"It was a very tense day, and I think that Captain Bob was a little bit like an expectant father outside the maternity ward. The captain of the Coast Guard District came down to observe. In some ways this was a historic event, because this boat is not only an icon to those of us who have grown up on these waters, but I think most people don't realize the amount of respect the Coast Guard has for Captain Bob and his abilities. His track record in sailing this vessel for fifty years places him far above many of the passenger vessel operators in our area. And I think that there's a reverence—let's put it that way—and it's well deserved.

"The test went very well except that about halfway through, I saw some results that didn't line up with my expectations. We got very nervous that something was going wrong. And it was only then that I realized that in numbering the barrels, the crane operator had confused the number six and number nine barrels, and I could actually see that in the results as I plotted them. When we sorted that out, everything lined right back up again. By the end of the day I was able to tell Captain Bob with high confidence that his memories of fifty years were entirely justified. The boat's vertical center of gravity and weight were pretty much unchanged. In the end it was a good day, but it was certainly a tense one."

Shenandoah and Douglas had passed the test. The exercise, which required many shipyard personnel and much heavy-duty machinery besides the crane, cost $30,000, which Douglas calls an unnecessary and "ruinous" expense.

Chapter 12

A Light Touch

Jamie Douglas, Robert Douglas's second son and the only one of the four boys who wanted to be a sea captain, became one, although time trimmed the scope of his childhood aspiration. "I thought I'd get my own square rigger. I was going to sail around Cape Horn in stormy seas." Did his dad want him to choose a seagoing career? "I have no idea. He likes the idea of Captain Douglas and Sons. That's what he says. He'd like to see it on the bumper of his truck, and he likes the fact that his family likes what he does."

From the 1960s to the present, *Shenandoah* has been for Douglas "my major enterprise forever." His welcoming table has overflowed with wife and family, with boats of all sorts, with restaurants and horses, with a host of seafaring friends, with an enormous correspondence with mariners and former guests aboard his schooner, with tugboats and former crew, and with folks who have attempted to follow in his footsteps. Still, notwithstanding all that has gathered about him, *Shenandoah* remains the centerpiece, what he yearned for and created.

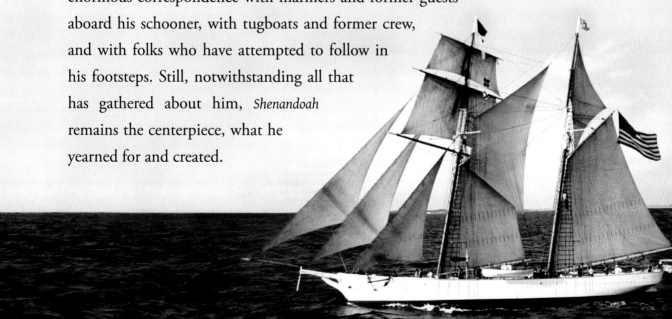

He did not urge his young sons to follow in his footsteps, but neither did he anxiously forbid them to "truck the mast," that is, to climb to the very top of the mainmast and sit on the cap. Nor did he tell his young crew to get down from there. Did his wife chafe at his obsessive focus on *Shenandoah*? "Well, I hardly think so," Jamie says. "I think that she supports him no matter what and allows him to do whatever he wants to do, when he wants to. And they have an incredible marriage. And he can basically go off-island right now and not tell her, and then call and tell her he's in Maine. And she'll go,

A Douglas family portrait. Left to right on the Coastwise Packet Company beach are Morgan, Robert, Charlene, Jamie, Brooke, and Rob.

'Oh, really? Hope you're having a great day. Come home—when are you coming?' And he'll say, 'I don't know. Sometime soon.' 'Fine. That's lovely,' she'll say. I see micromanaging between people who don't trust each other—well, that doesn't exist in their relationship."

Likewise in his relationships with his crew: "To them, I think, he did it by example," Jamie says. "I can recall a meeting or two a year when he would sit down with the crew and say—it was very short, there wasn't a lot of paper involved. He'd say, 'This is what I want to do. This is what I want to see.' And it was simple, like: 'Never fall asleep on watch. You don't come out here and play around. This is a serious operation.' And I think he led by example. They saw, definitely for the first thirty years plus, that he would be out there. He'd go to work on the topsides. He'd do the painting. So, they saw it. They knew and learned rather quickly what his expectations were because they saw him doing it. I think that's how he communicated."

Douglas's four boys sailed with their father and Charlene as infants. Two small, cleverly designed deckhouses were added, complementary to the original deck arrangement with curving roofs and sliding doors, and nicknamed "doghouses." The mate moved out of the captain's cabin and took one of the new accommodations, a babysitter took the other, and Charlene lived in the captain's cabin with Douglas, although Douglas also shared his cabin with his father for a late-in-the-season week or two on many occasions.

As the boys grew up, they worked as deckhands, answering to and learning from the mate and the crew. "When I was working on *Shenandoah*," Jamie recalls, "you spoke to those guys, not to Dad. There were a lot of guys back then who came up from deckhand to be three, four, five, six years as bosun then mate. Guys came up underneath them, so there was a lot of overlap of experience. It was really organic. That's how 'the way we do it' got passed along."

Asked if he ever wanted to be a sea captain, Morgan Douglas, now 44, answers, "No. I hate sailing offshore. I got sick. And I was terrible at it. The hardcore, dangerous-type sailing, I'll save that for kite surfing." He, along with Rob Douglas, the oldest son and holder of a world speed record, known in exalted circles as the world's fastest sailor, are competitive kite surfers.

"I'm the opposite of an offshore sailor," Morgan says. "I grew up sailing each day from point A to point B, spending each night on the anchor, and planning the next day, whether it was just following orders as a crewmember on the *Shenandoah* or doing it myself as captain of *Alabama*, that's the type of sailing I enjoy. I didn't like the blue water, open-ocean stuff. I got a little taste of it. I can answer a phone call when one of Ralph Packer's tugboat captains needs some crew, like a short-notice crewmember for a trip. I can go do that. Stepping on board somebody else's boat is a totally different deal. But I never wanted to be a sea captain."

Morgan is the manager of Black Dog Tall Ships, a position he has held since 2005, after a long stint learning the restaurant business at the Black Dog Tavern. "For me and my brothers, our relationship with the Black Dog all kind of started around working for the Tavern Company in 2001. I did that for a few years, and it was really just a normal kind of routine for my dad. Sometimes he would be trying to find someone to staff or captain or work on the boats. And my turn was up. 'What are you doing this summer?' 'Oh, right now, I'm working in the restaurants, learning the ropes inside the kitchen, managing the restaurants, learning how to do that.' 'Well, I need a captain for *Alabama*.' That's really where Black Dog Tall Ships started for me, and it was an opportunity to come back to work for a different part of the company, but one that was the only job I had prior to working for the Black Dog Tavern Company. The Tavern was the only job I had ever known from the time I was probably 14 or 15, all the way through when I graduated college, which was when I was 24 years old. And I've done it ever since. The beauty of this seasonal job, I think, is that it allows me to have the best office, the best work spot, because I've done all the other things working in the restaurant, which is still the hardest work I ever did, in terms of just the grind, the routine. Just the pace of it. And I get to look at my dad's collections, all around. This is where I get to come to work every day and be involved in something that I get to see and touch every day, too."

What had been Robert Douglas and *Shenandoah* in 1960, the pure though astonishingly demanding pairing of one 28-year-old and his dream, became in 1970 and over the following few years a Douglas family enterprise. Fortunately for Douglas, whose "major enterprise forever" was never to become other than *Shenandoah*, Charlene Douglas and their four boys embraced the changes, demands, and challenges that Douglas himself left them to oversee. Today, Brooke Douglas runs the Coastwise company marina, Morgan Douglas runs Black Dog Tall Ships, Jamie Douglas is captain of the schooner *Alabama*, and Rob, the eldest son, is a board member of the company that is the new owner of the Black Dog Tavern business.

Rob, now 50, has been chief executive of Black Dog Enterprises for more than twenty years. "I didn't throw baseballs with my dad," he says. "I didn't do the typical stuff that my friends did with their dads. I never went fishing a day with my dad. That just wasn't something we did. But I grew up with him daily. I spent every summer with him, 24 hours a day, six days a week on *Shenandoah*. I mean, we'd sail the boat together, and I would be at the wheel and he was always there, but in a way he wasn't. If I wanted him there, he would be there. He wouldn't grab me and say, 'Hey! Let's go fishing.' He would say to me, 'Hey, let's sail the Bahama boat,' or 'Hey, let's go ashore at Padanaram and go see Grandma,' or 'Hey, let's go get some ice cream at Cuttyhunk.' So, it was different in that way. And I didn't realize it at the time. I realized it when I got a little bit older. But I always looked up to him.

"I would climb the rigging of *Shenandoah,* and this eternal optimist would look up at me as I'm sitting on the top of the foremast, 94 feet above the water, with total confidence, and he'd maybe wave, maybe not. I'd come back down on deck—not many words were spoken. I had this freedom to do things that as a dad today, there's no way I would let my kids do. But he allowed me that freedom to do things that definitely contributed to who I am today, a freedom to make decisions. So, like I said, he didn't throw the baseball with me, but he did some pretty serious things. And when I look at my life—I turned 50 two weeks ago—I became a pilot because I had listened to my dad's stories. He told many stories on *Shenandoah* in summertime. I would ask him about flying, and I would hear him talk to his flying buddy Norman Gingrass about flying. So, I was around this aviation talk, and when the opportunity was presented to me, I wanted to fly airplanes. I ended up doing it in a different capacity, for a commercial cargo company. I got all my licenses. And then sailing has been a massive part of my life. It's funny. It's similar to Dad, the passion, but in a totally different vehicle. Dad will tell you he's stuck

Robert Douglas in his workshop on the Vineyard Haven waterfront. To the untutored visitor it may seem cluttered and disorganized. To Douglas, it is the resource he has stocked and catalogued with anything he may ever need to keep his fleet operating. This painting is the work of Eleanor Lanahan, for 31 years the partner of Robert's brother John, who died in January 2022.

in 1870. That's where he thinks the world should have stopped. That's where he thinks technology should have stopped. I love the modern materials that allowed me to do 55 knots and set a world record on a kite surfer. I'm very connected to him through aviation and sailing, and the exposure that I got on *Shenandoah* and with Dad has brought me to where I am and how I am today."

In 2016, Rob Douglas began to encourage the Black Dog Tavern company's shareholders—all family members—to consider a new direction for the business.

"I think Dad's age was a part of it, but also because the brothers are all shareholders in the company. And we were starting now to have families of our own, and with that came different pathways in life. So, I think in 2016 we started to really kick that can and try to flesh out what the future could look like. My idea for the first step was, 'Okay, what do we have today?' So, we had an evaluation process done with accountants, and we took a look at it. And then you get kind of a market number, which they can do in various ways without actually going to market, which is the ultimate way of determining a price. But you can get an idea, which we did. And then within that idea or that price, we looked at—you know, there are shares in the company and also real estate in the company—what would a sale look like? Would it be just the business and its assets? Would it be the real estate? There were different ways we could play it, based on what the shareholders thought was more attractive to them.

"I got diagnosed with cancer in 2016, and that nudged me toward a different mindset than a lot of the shareholders because for a while I was looking at biopsies and chemotherapy and radiation, and of course that's a time in your life when you take a little half-halt and say, 'Holy smoke, what am I doing?' I have a good feeling that the stress I was under from running the business for twenty years contributed to an environment where cancer had a better chance of affecting me, so that made me take a fresh look at a bunch of things. And that's when we started the process."

Rob and Brooke, the youngest son, had been only peripherally involved with the operation of the two Black Dog schooners. Morgan and Jamie operated the vessels and oversaw the passenger business. Life interfered with the planning discussions, and no decisions were made until 2020.

"Still, I'm 50. I have three kids. Jamie's 49 and has two kids. Morgan's 46 and has one. So, in 2020, when the pandemic came along, I think it pushed that idea of selling the company or part of the company back onto the front stage. As CEO, I presented it again to the shareholders as a time to take a look at the opportunity. We owned all the real estate and all the business assets, and that's good. We've been doing that successfully for many years. But it felt a little undiversified, if that's a word. I felt like we needed to spread out and take a few chips off the table.

"I wouldn't call myself a pessimist, but I'm the exact opposite of my dad in that respect. His world is golden all the time, and I think that's a real strength. I'm jealous of the fact that I can't live in that world. I kind of think I'm in the world to balance that at the company level and inside the family. I felt like, 'You know, we've done this for fifty years.' To use Dad's analogy, we were sailing every day. We were leaving the anchor. We were doing our jobs. But if you play and sail along the coast long enough, things can happen that you haven't planned for and that are not necessarily comfortable. So, in a nutshell, I wanted to diversify, and an opportunity came along for us to do that in 2020."

As it happened, there was a buyer at hand. Dan Pucillo, of Falmouth, Massachusetts, had been the chief operating officer of Black Dog for almost twenty years and knew the business intimately. He and Rob had worked together to grow and diversify the enterprise, expanding it from $10 million in annual revenues toward $30 million. The sale of Black Dog to Pucillo does not include the restaurant property and the adjacent former

Coastwise Packet Company property and dock. Pucillo will lease the restaurant property and all the other Black Dog outlets up and down the East Coast. He now owns the Black Dog Cafe property on State Road in Tisbury. The Douglas family retained their shares in the business.

The creation of the Black Dog Tavern at the beginning of the 1970s appeared to signal a promising expansion of Douglas's foundational concept, which was *Shenandoah* and only her, the sole promontory on his horizon. That busy decade featured other fresh outbreaks of varied and later cherished new interests, but sparkling and alluring as each of them became, the fixed star remained what it had always been.

Chapter 13

A Half-Century's Voyage

WHO AT THE TIME could have been persuaded that 29-year-old Robert Douglas was committing himself to anything but certain folly when, in 1961, he gave Harvey Gamage an earnest thousand dollars to hold a place for *Shenandoah* in the South Bristol builder's shed? Havilah Hawkins, Douglas's friend and mentor, had run sailing excursions for paying passengers in two antique, repurposed coasting schooners for more than a decade before building a brand-new vessel, which he and his family operated in the Maine windjammer trade for another 35 years. Douglas could claim no such experience of designing, building, or operating a passenger vessel under sail. And yet, commanding mostly teenaged crews, none of them seasoned mariners or square-rig veterans, he logged 56 successful summers as *Shenandoah's* sole master.

"Doubtless there is a providence, some special planetary influence for the express purpose of protecting youth from the consequences of its own folly," wrote Errol Flynn in the quote that is this book's epigraph, but Douglas relied on more than providence.

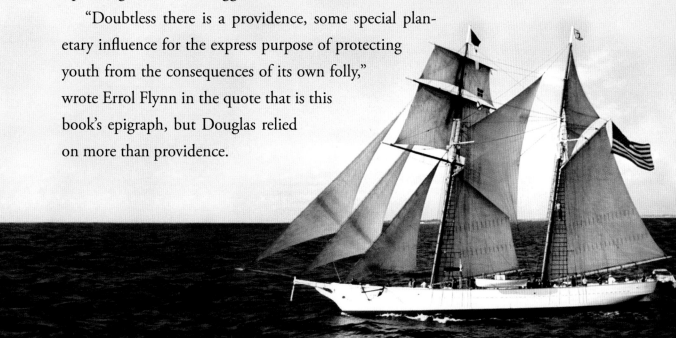

Shenandoah crosses the finish line in the 1971 Vineyard Schooner Race.

Conversations with crewmembers—recent and long-ago—and letters from passengers make clear that, from the start, Douglas was guided by a deep understanding of his vessel. He knew when to accept her limits, when to press her to perform, and what she needed from her people. "This vessel," Douglas told his son Jamie, "creates a framework." He expected his sons, the sailors, and the experience itself to fill that frame.

"The commitment to doing things right and learning and being knowledgeable was part of the spirit of the thing," said Matthew Stackpole, deckhand, bosun, and mate in the 1960s. "That's what it came down to. And that comes from the top. Bob never lectured us on his expectations. He just demonstrated what was expected by the way he did things, and the early crew—Dan Goodenough was one of them—set the tone. A passenger once told Dan that he had a great last name for a ship's cook, and we used to tease him about that because, on *Shenandoah,* good enough was never enough.

"Sail handling comes to mind—sheeting the sails and stowing the topsails, lowers, and jibs. We had to have a neat, compact harbor furl. The bunt is always a challenge in a square sail—getting it spread out enough—and if it wasn't done right, we'd say, 'There's a baby in the bunting,' meaning a bulge in the middle, and you'd have to do it again until you got it right. It was that way with everything; you did it right or you did it again. And we were sailors, not yachtsmen."

Morgan Douglas reflected on his father's family leadership practices in a conversation in the jam-packed Black Dog Tall Ships office, a warren unlike any a visitor would expect to find at the headquarters of a thriving, multifaceted, multimillion-dollar 50-year-old business. Phones and faxes sounded off, and interruptions were frequent. Morgan describes his father in terms similar to those used by former crewmembers.

"You know, my dad's involvement in the office is pretty low," he says. "Aboard *Shenandoah* it was different, of course, but even when preparing me to be her captain he wasn't long on specifics. It was more like, 'Son, here's what we're doing, here's what the boat can do and what it can't do, and let's talk about it, and let's get you ready for this.' My old man did not like lecturing anybody, whether it was a passenger, the crew, or his own kids."

Then how did he teach and inspire all the people who became crewmembers for him? "The same thing. It's through repetition and people being on board that boat. But until recently, the last ten years, we never put time into training a replacement captain, because my dad's relationship with that boat is like—I mean, I talk about it with some of my brothers now. He doesn't talk about *Shenandoah* as 'she.' I remember one time we were in France at this kite-surfing event, and it was blowing 40 knots onto the beach, and we see this little boat sailing upwind toward a harbor up the beach. And Jamie, joking around, said, 'Hey, Dad, what would the *Shenandoah* be like out there today?' And he said, 'Well, I can't sail to weather in 40 knots.' The *Shenandoah* is him. He refers to the boat as 'I.' So, he wasn't training up other people."

Several of the most highly regarded former *Shenandoah* crew have become merchant mariners, chief officers on freighters and tankers, even square riggers, around the world, and have made their lives on Martha's Vineyard. Others have followed non-marine pursuits but have likewise made their lives and careers on the Vineyard, seduced by their youthful experience aboard *Shenandoah*. "But," Morgan says, "you don't get too many Billy Mabies, Scott Youngs, or Ian Ridgeways who are put on a different path through their lives by this program."

Scott Young summered with his family on Cape Cod, and sailing, often with another family group in a 36-foot Crosby cat yawl, was a big part of the vacation activities. "And I remember seeing the schooner in the late 1960s, and I was after that experience from the beginning. I wrote Bob a couple of letters in the winter when I was sixteen." He kept writing until he got a job. He docked yachts and sold ice at the Coastwise marina, then finally got a berth as galley boy aboard the schooner.

Marine historian Howard Chapelle had taken note of the handsome sculpted eagle that decorated the bowsprit of each of the Treasury Department's flashy revenue cutters. Shenandoah carried a decorative billethead on her bow until Travis Fulton, a Colorado sculptor, moved to the Vineyard in the mid-1970s and spent several months creating this handsome and unique eagle just for *Shenandoah*.

"I found that there wasn't anything that was unworthy of attention on that boat. Everything was just so. Everything was done promptly and correctly. You were led to understand by Bob, by the mate, by the bosun, that this is the way to do it. Just absorption. Just suck it up, like a sponge. Sixteen years old. I had to figure out how to wash dishes for forty people first. That's the first step. My favorite story that I still crank out: Bob makes an appearance in the galley when we've been chugging along for a week or more, maybe two weeks. I hadn't really had any kind of word with him up to then. So he comes down to the galley and says to me, 'Well, what do you think of this work so far?,' and meanwhile he's checking the tops of the grills and such. And it was like everything else, you know? You were led to understand that if you got your ass out of the galley at a reasonable time, come up the street with us, you know, if we're in Nantucket or wherever. Like that. So, I had a gang. It was my first real gang, I would say. It was good for me. For me it was a place that I was accepted, and I felt like I belonged."

Young's father had died when Scott was ten. His mother rented summer places on the Vineyard as Scott's seasonal preoccupation with *Shenandoah* endured, and she later bought a house on the island. "I think she followed me here to the Vineyard, in a way, in a quiet way."

Young remembers Douglas greeting the week's guests on Sunday evenings in *Shenandoah*'s kerosene lamp – lit saloon. Until that moment, *Shenandoah*'s master would be a barely seen mystery to the passengers. "My memory of the Sunday night talks is of puzzled passengers saying, 'What did he say? What was that?' And one of the great breakthroughs was in my second or third year as mate. Robbie was always busy, so was Jamie, and Charlene was six directions at once, and getting down to the dock for a thirty-minute orientation on Sunday night was becoming a hardship for Bob. So, I kind of took over the duty, graduating from explaining how the toilets worked to giving the full lecture.

"A lot of that orientation was just anticipating the usual questions in my little set piece. I'd say things like, 'This is what we're going to try to do. And it's a really cool kind of vessel, so you're going to need to help. And when you help, we're going to prompt you, but. . . .' I wasn't very erudite. I just covered the bases so people could feel comfortable. A lot of people, you know, they're like 'Wh-wh-what did I sign up for?'"

Young left college, and during what would have been his junior and senior years, he worked on *Shenandoah* until October, then began work on coastwise tugboats in the Chesapeake winters. And after several years operating tugboats and other vessels on both coasts, he bought some Vineyard land, got married, had children, built a house next to another merchant mariner, and became a housebuilder.

Bill Mabie, a *Shenandoah* mate for four seasons, made a career as a merchant marine officer on large tankers and cargo ships. He shipped eight or more years on Exxon vessels in Cameroon and Angola and spent months in Antarctica. He also served as master of the 148-foot barquentine *Regina Maris.* He too made his home on the Vineyard.

Mabie's introduction to *Shenandoah* was similar to that of other young people who came to serve on the boat. "It would have been 1970," he remembers. "We rented a house on Nantucket, and I just happened to be standing downtown, you know, like at Fort Apache [a nickname for the Nantucket Boat Basin] when the *Shenandoah* came sailing in. It was a pretty impressive sight. I was, like, 'Wow! That's cool.'

"When I got out of high school I got a job, first on the dock. I worked there summers in college and then kind of didn't leave. Mom wanted me to be a doctor or lawyer, something like that. My dad . . . well okay, so I've got, I don't know, five generations of my family who've had master's licenses."

Shenandoah reaches before a smart breeze on the starboard beam, everything but the fisherman's staysail set and drawing handsomely.

What is consistent too is Mabie's description of his experience aboard Douglas's schooner. "Basically, it's a big-time learning experience," he says. "And it wasn't like Bob saying, 'Okay at 9 o'clock we're having class.' No, you'd get thrown together with people you didn't know, and you'd build these lifelong friendships, it turns out. And the camaraderie, the esprit de corps, and the pride in what you're doing is a little bit bigger than just flipping burgers. Bob is not necessarily a good teacher, but the platform that he'd created with that boat and the marina, the whole program, was an excellent teacher. When I was working there, all the knowledge was passed down. It wasn't something you learned in a nice, gentle, pat-on-the-back fashion. It was, 'Hey, dumbass, this is what you do! How many times I gotta tell you?' Like figuring out which way the wind's blowing when you dump the coal ash, as one simple example. It's all important."

There is an uncounted cohort of passengers, adults and children, salty seagoing tall-ship types, crew who discovered and attached themselves to *Shenandoah* and the Douglas enterprises in one fashion or another, and the small multitude who came and then got on with their lives, taking with themselves no more than a fading memory of a sunny, windy week under sail. Among the voters of the town of Tisbury on Martha's Vineyard, once known as Holmes Hole and including the waterfront village of Vineyard Haven, *Shenandoah* has been, since her arrival in 1964, a municipal treasure, a totem really. Her popularity and the high regard in which Douglas was held as her master, however, did not launch a political career for him, though he tried.

Douglas ran several times for one of the three seats on the town board of selectmen, but his earnest efforts were unavailing. At each year's annual meet-the-candidates night, Douglas soliloquized about the history of the harbor where his schooners were moored and where, at the end of the nineteenth century and beginning of the twentieth, dozens of schooners had stopped, so many that a Seaman's Bethel was built on the edge of the harbor to serve the sailors' spiritual needs. He deprecated the Steamship Authority for its relentless expansion along the harbor front and its ever-larger ferries and their more frequent car- and passenger-carrying trips to and from the mainland.

His opponents campaigned on tax rates, school budgets, slowing the rate of summer home construction, the need to improve the town school, the flooding of the Beach Road and its adjacent properties every time a northeast storm tormented the island, and zoning rules—nonexistent until 1974—that were either too restrictive or not restrictive enough, depending on whether you wanted to build a house or your nearby neighbor did. Douglas knew how discouraging a headwind could be, and after five attempts he left town politics to others.

If his hallmark was not going to be the municipal refashioning—old-fashioning may be a more accurate term—of his beloved, adopted hometown, there was a way in which he and *Shenandoah* would, over time, help recast Vineyard Haven harbor. Douglas—or perhaps *Shenandoah*—is often credited with sparking what has become a wooden boat harbor of refuge against the overwhelming storm of fiberglass sailboats and craft made of even stranger materials, neither organic nor natural. As Randall Peffer wrote in the January/February 2021 edition of *WoodenBoat* magazine, "Over the past 45 years, the port has changed from a commercial harbor and ferry terminal to the homeport of a trove of superbly built and lovingly maintained wooden vessels. Today, Vineyard Haven, less than five miles across Nantucket Sound from Cape Cod, is nothing less than a visual feast for everyone who loves boats."

Nat Benjamin of Gannon and Benjamin Marine Railway on the harbor shore—designer, builder, or rebuilder of 72 plank-on-frame boats over the years, has a slightly different take. "You know, when we came here in the early 1970s, the wooden boat renaissance in New England had begun but on a very low scale. If anyone gets the credit, it might be Jonathan Wilson. He had just started *WoodenBoat* magazine. John Gardner was writing those columns for the *National Fisherman* magazine. And anyone who was interested in wooden boats was reading those magazines—along with the Hornblower novels and all that stuff. That, as much as anything, kicked off the wooden boat renaissance, if you can call it that. And locally, Ross [Gannon] and I got together, and we both had old boats. We were scrambling to haul our own boats, and going to Jerry Grant's railway, over in Edgartown, but there was no really good solution. We were both talking about, 'Gosh, if we only had a little railway here.' I had hauled an old schooner that I sailed in Morocco at a very simple railway in Spanish Morocco, and I envisioned that type of operation here—a simple railway and a dock and a gin pole, pretty much what we have here today.

"I don't think it was any one person. You know, Ralph Packer, just maintaining that whole commercial end of the harbor, was instrumental in keeping this working waterfront alive. Our little operation contributed too. We started designing and building new boats, and that was something new here, because before it had just been repairing old ones like the *Shenandoah* and *Alabama* and old catboats and things like that. So, I guess we're responsible for the yacht side of the renaissance. But Bob, he certainly can claim ownership of the traditional, historical side of the marine scene here, with everything that he does. He sort of eschewed anything new at first, until he saw us building new boats that looked traditional.

"But Douglas is a bigger-than-life figure, not in the wooden yacht-building community but in the attention he's attracted to Vineyard Haven. *Shenandoah* is the flagship of Vineyard Haven, if not Martha's Vineyard, grounding everything else that has happened here. That vessel is just a stunning example of what could be done in the twentieth century."

Chapter 14

A New Schooner

As a young man, Robert Douglas might have been mistaken for the movie version of Fletcher Christian, but he aged as *Shenandoah* did. By his ninth decade he more closely resembled Benjamin Franklin. His slow, painful walk, gnarled, thickened hands, and ruddy face belong to a ship's master who has stood long watches at the wheel over the "green and merry seas."

In 2019 Douglas once again found himself skirmishing with Coast Guard licensing authorities, just as he had more than a half-century earlier in a moment of greater jeopardy, when the newly launched *Shenandoah* needed a Coast Guard license to carry paying passengers. He and the passenger-vessel inspectors he calls, without conviction, his "Coast Guard friends" had often differed through the intervening years as to the condition of the vessel and her suitability for her trade. Now, the inspectors had once again demanded that Douglas rebuild *Shenandoah's* stern circle, the rounded back end of the vessel rising around and above the sternpost.

The red oak in that area had developed pockets of rot over time, as red oak insists on doing. Douglas knew that a stern-circle rebuild would be needed again one day—it was a critical support for the considerable weight of *Shenandoah*'s diesel-powered yawl boat,

Shenandoah's master is, today, not the 35-year-old who made a dream come true, but a 90-year-old attending to his correspondence and projecting a Ben Franklin aura.

for one thing—but he didn't think it was needed immediately, and he chafed at the demand. *Shenandoah*, he believed, was so heavily built that the vessel's structural integrity was not at risk. In support of his assertion, he offered a comparison of the longevity of the red oak used in *Shenandoah*'s original construction, 1964 – 2007, or 43 years, and of the white oak used by the Boothbay shipyard in its reconstruction of *Shenandoah*'s stern circle, 2007 – 2021, or 11 years. "So, it was not the fault of the red oak," he says.

The signs of deterioration were not yet alarming; there was no visible sagging or flattening of *Shenandoah*'s designed sheer, a discouraging condition called "hogging." He pleaded for two years of relief from the Coast Guard's demand. He argued that he couldn't afford the repair the Coast Guard was demanding. "You will put me out of business," he told the inspectors. And that is what happened.

"Progression" is the word Douglas uses to describe the unfolding of his life. It is as if nothing has been a calculated choice. He believes that Martha's Vineyard led him to sailboats, that his attachment to the Maine windjammers led to the *Bounty,* that *Bounty* led to *Joe Lane,* and that she led to *Shenandoah,* which led to Black Dog Tavern and its derivative businesses, to Charlene, to his family, and to *Alabama.* In his overstuffed, labyrinthine office, Douglas keeps the plans for two sailing vessels. One is *Shenandoah.* The second is the steel topsail schooner school ship he envisioned in 1970 and has dwelt upon, fiddling with her design, ever since. For more than half a century the new steel schooner has never been out of his mind. In 1970 she was a notion. As of 2021, her realization is the goal of a devoted team of supporters who expect what they all refer to as "the steel schooner" will be under sail with student sailors in the next few years. Larger than *Shenandoah*, her design, with the help of collaborators at Halter Marine, is an offspring of *Shenandoah* and of Irving Johnson's famous world-girdling *Yankee*.

Shenandoah and *Alabama* (after she was rebuilt and placed in service) have offered a learning experience under sail to more than 7,000 children. Deborah L. Hale, then a teacher at the Tisbury School, one of Martha's Vineyard's five grammar schools, described the student experience in a letter to Douglas that she also sent to the editors of the two Martha's Vineyard newspapers on September 8, 1996. Hers is a common assessment of the experience young people have commemorated in drawings and letters to Captain Douglas over the years:

Sheer thrills. Student passengers leap from the main crosstrees.

> The *Shenandoah* captain, crew, cook, and teachers aboard provide a forum for the children to learn about the sea in a hands-on environment. This experience gave the children the opportunity to experience and learn about their own heritage. As a result of this experience these children will have a respect for the sea and how the survival of those who live and work by and on the sea depends upon the strength of the group as well as the individual. As children growing up on the island, many have never had the opportunity to learn about the Vineyard seafaring world, and this trip gave them exposure in a structured and caring environment. The rhythm of life on the sea was one that all of the children embraced. They learned, without being told, the importance of working as a group and how one person's actions impact another. The Tisbury class of 2000 not only developed as a group but as individuals as well. There were acts of true bravery happening at every moment of the day. Through climbing the rigging, swinging on

the ropes, climbing the chains, swimming around the *Shenandoah*, walking on the beaches with no shoes, to working through frustrations of making a perfect Flemish coil, every child aboard had the opportunity to do something new, each to their own level of development with the complete support of the rest of the group. I was amazed by it all.

These ten-year-olds had a true 'Outward Bound' experience. It was filled with the joys of singing, learning knots and the parts of the boat, playing new card games, hide and seek, Balderdash, and was one of the richest experiences of my life. It was a joy to see all of the children grow. I can't thank Captain Douglas enough for all that you do for all of the children of Martha's Vineyard by making this experience a possibility. The crew was fabulous. They were clear and kind to all of the children. The cook provided us with delicious food and was a humorous teacher as well. And lastly, you taught the children about respect, patience, and the beauty of the sea.

In 2019, stymied by the Coast Guard, Douglas at last considered offers to take *Shenandoah* off his hands. One came from a Georgia park owner who proposed to display the schooner on land, fully rigged, in a building he would erect that would be tall enough to accommodate her 94-foot masts and be climate-controlled to halt her deterioration. Ultimately, Douglas could not see how that idea would fit with the particular progression he had in mind.

The offer that fit best came from the Foundation for Underway Experiential Learning (FUEL), a 501(c)(3) nonprofit enterprise founded in 2016 by Ian Ridgeway and Casey Blum. Both are experienced captains who learned their trade aboard *Shenandoah* and *Alabama*. For them, starting a nonprofit was out of the ordinary course of events as they had experienced it, but at the same time a clear next step in the progression that Douglas had in mind. "We've done everything that starting a nonprofit entails," Blum said in 2020. "Early on that meant managing the logistics of recruiting board members, starting to get donations, learning about fundraising, and that whole side of things. Now we're entering the operating phase, running the programming. So, my attention has shifted a lot more now into program design and implementation."

In September 2020, at the age of 88, Robert Douglas donated *Shenandoah*, valued at $2 million, to FUEL. It made perfect sense in his progression. FUEL would extend and expand the school ship mission that had begun and matured as Black Dog Tall Ships twenty years after *Shenandoah* was launched. And the long-term plan calls for FUEL to build the steel topsail schooner Douglas designed all those years ago.

Before FUEL's programming could get underway, *Shenandoah*'s stern circle had to be rebuilt. The Mystic Seaport Shipyard, known for its high-quality and historically responsible work on historic vessels such as the whaleship *Charles W. Morgan,* did the work, including additional repairs and upgrades, at a cost of roughly $300,000. *Shenandoah* also needed a new suit of sails—a $75,000 investment. Returned to her Vineyard Haven mooring in July 2021, *Shenandoah* loaded school children for the first cruise of her fifty-seventh year. Two grants made that possible.

The United States Coast Guard document transferring ownership of *Shenandoah* from Robert S. Douglas and Coastwise Packet Company to the nonprofit Foundation for Underway Experiential Learning (FUEL) on April 21, 2021.

"We were fortunate to receive a $100,000 grant from the Martha's Vineyard Youth Collaborative and a $20,000 grant from the Martha's Vineyard Community Endowment," Blum explained. "The application processes were rigorous. They wanted to know exactly how many island young people we planned to serve in summer of 2021 and how long we thought we could keep *Shenandoah* running. They knew about the long-term plan to build a new ship, so they made the grant to have the work done on *Shenandoah* with the understanding that we'll operate it for the next two to five years as we work toward building the new ship.

"FUEL's mission is personal development for its student-sailors. There are all sorts of lessons to be learned, and there is academic rigor that you can focus on when you're out on board the boat. From my experience being out there, and through the programs I've worked for in the outdoor education industry, the magic that happens is in the personal development and growth. Leadership skills, conflict resolution, and problem solving—those are the kinds of things that are inherent in being on board and under sail for young people—especially the development of leadership skills."

Harry Dickerson, a retired professor of veterinary medicine at the University of Georgia, grew up in Connecticut and spent summers in the Martha's Vineyard town of Oak Bluffs. A FUEL board member, he can trace his commitment to the nonprofit through generations of his own family. "There used to be a train that came up from Saybrook, Connecticut to Woods Hole every Friday," he recalls, "and then every Sunday night it would go back. And you'd see all these little kids on the steamboat wharf going 'Bye, Daddy. Bye, Daddy.' All these guys that were pasty white going back to their jobs in the city, and their sun-browned wives and kids would stay on the island. I was one of those kids—I think my father bought the place in Oak Bluffs when I was 12 years old. And I was 15 when *Shenandoah* first made her appearance in Vineyard Haven, and—probably like a lot of people—the sight of that schooner just fascinated me. The rigging, the masts, the white hull, the square rig—I was enthralled right away. She was unique, so magnificent when you saw her sailing in Vineyard Sound or off the beach there in Oak Bluffs. We'd be sitting there and we'd see her go by, and she was just amazing to me. So I really wanted to be part of that." In 1967, a high school senior, he wrote Douglas to ask for a job and then visited him for what turned out to be a day-long interview that began in Douglas's Vineyard Haven kitchen. He got a job, not as a deckhand, but as so many before him had, working on the Coastwise marina dock. The following summer he was elevated to galley boy and then deckhand aboard the schooner.

Dickerson grew to regard his experience as especially meaningful and useful, worth extending to the next generation of his own family. Seeing how uncertain his son was about college and the future, he encouraged the boy to apply to Douglas for a job, as Dickerson himself had done. "I just sort of laid it out there for him, and he jumped at it. Bob takes chances on people."

"The memories that I made really resonated with me," Dickerson says. "Even the smells bring back those memories today, the smell of pine tar and paint. Those things are vivid in my memory, and I am rewarded by them today. I can remember one summer when I was on *Shenandoah,* my mother was in the Oak Bluffs house and I went to visit with her. And she said, 'You know, you smell just like your grandfather used to smell.' He had been a professional sailor in Maine. Aboard *Shenandoah* we'd been sluicing the forestays with pine tar and turpentine, which is kind of neat. My senses were open to all sorts of experiences. Everything was new. The smells, the sights, climbing up in the rigging, the challenge of that. It still resonates so much with me today."

Eleven years old, Ian Ridgeway arrived on Martha's Vineyard with his mother after a period of turmoil in his family's mainland life. He attended the Tisbury grammar school and spent a summer week aboard *Shenandoah* with his classmates. For him, that week did the trick. He began hanging out at the Coastwise dock on Saturday afternoons after that week's passengers were disembarked and the schooner's crew began the cleaning, maintenance, and preparation for the passengers who would board on Sunday evening. Soon, he was helping with the weekend chores, an ad hoc member of the crew. Next, he asked Douglas if he could spend a week aboard—should there ever be room for supercargo—and was rewarded with an invitation. In 2002 and for the next four years,

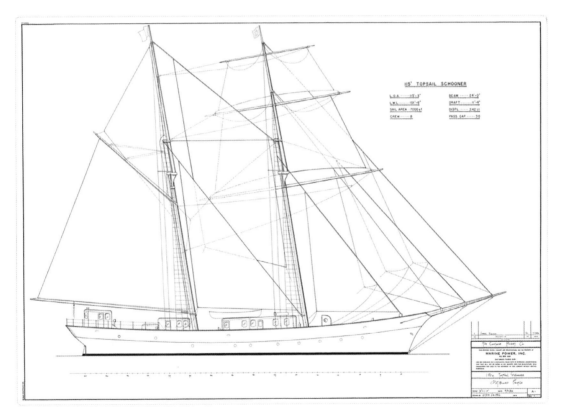

Looking ahead. Here is a profile view of the steel schooner Douglas began musing over in 1970. Her construction is the chief goal of the FUEL nonprofit to which Douglas donated *Shenandoah* in 2021. She will be bigger than *Shenandoah* and heavier, wider, deeper, and more capacious. As she is envisioned, she will make school ship training a year-round enterprise.

he served as mate on *Shenandoah*, and later as captain of *Alabama*. In 2021, he was not only the co-founder of FUEL but the captain of *Shenandoah* as she made her first cruises without Douglas at the helm.

With *Shenandoah* sailing under the FUEL flag in 2022, Douglas has his unbuilt steel schooner on his mind. She will, after all, be the yearned-for next progression in his long life. Until she leaves the dock one day, gets sail on, and sets her course for—well, it's anyone's guess where—she is a mystery, and he is easily drawn into a discussion of what the new vessel will be and his fervent hope for FUEL's success. Of course, he knows all the new schooner's attributes: what she looks like in two dimensions, her length, her weight, her rig. She is a lot bigger than *Yankee* and even *Shenandoah*, displacing 248 tons to *Shenandoah*'s 170. Part of the difference is attributable to an increase in beam from 24 to 26 feet. Her sail area, he guesses, will be greater than *Shenandoah*'s 7,000 square feet, but he doesn't know that for sure, nor can he be sure she will sail as fast as *Shenandoah*. He shudders at the criticism directed at some unfortunate sailing vessels, that their "best point of sail is hove-to."

He muses that her greater weight will add power, especially when tacking. "If I had to say what one thing I'd change about *Shenandoah*, now that I've sailed her for fifty-five years, I'd give her more displacement. She'd have more weight to give her more way on when she tacks. That would be important. She's marginal now. I've got to sail around with topsails. If anything, she's got too much windage for her mass. What makes a boat tack? Momentum. And if you've got too much windage slowing the tack, your momentum doesn't last long enough to overcome it. I think the steel schooner will tack better, and that will make her faster upwind." Strictly restraining his fathomless devotion to what he looks forward to as the next step in his life's progression, he adds, "It will be very interesting to see how she turns out."

Acknowledgments

THIS BOOK WAS MY wife Molly's idea. She has lots of good ideas, and I have a deplorable but instinctive inclination to bedevil each one of them with questions, objections, and doubts. But not this time. This time I gratefully, enthusiastically, and immediately joined up. My gratitude begins with her but encompasses many others.

Aware that the world has hurried relentlessly, heedlessly on, leaving nearly everything Captain Robert S. Douglas cherishes discarded in tatters along the long winding trail, I worried aloud to friends that telling the captain's story might be neither necessary nor desirable. What I heard from most was some gratifying variation of, "It's a great idea, and you're the only one who can write it." I knew that last part was a crock, but I was encouraged nevertheless.

It was easy to decode and discard the common view of Douglas, which was, "He's been sailing *Shenandoah* around for half a century, what more is there to know about him?" There was a lot more, and I knew it.

Aged newspaperman that I am, I was reminded of the expression from the business's salad days that everyone has a story, some lively, some common, but each unique. Some of those stories are remarkable for what we thought we knew but did not. Douglas's story is one of those. So, here we are.

Bedrock thanks go to the Foundation for Underway Experiential Learning (FUEL), whose board of directors—especially Ian Ridgeway, Casey Blum, John McDonald, and Harry Dickerson—agreed to underwrite this effort. Douglas's story, by itself, accounts for the enormous commitment FUEL has made to carry on and enlarge what he began.

Robert Douglas is the definitive edition of the encyclopedia of himself. Names, dates, places, boats, sailors, friends, friends who've disappointed, friends accomplished beyond measure, friends in whom he has seen something they hadn't noticed in themselves, relentless exasperation with certain authorities, even the wind direction and strength on the day he anchored in a harbor he had never visited before and would never visit again: all this and more is available, page after virtual page, in his 90-year-old memory. He was unstintingly generous with his time and attention, answering question after question for hours on end and sometimes answering the same question twice. Charlene Douglas also generously accommodated my interruptions and requests that certainly fractured her very busy days.

John Bruce Douglas of Burlington, Vermont, died in January 2022 at age 84, leaving Bob the only one of James and Grace Douglas's four sons still alive. Despite being gravely ill, John made time only weeks before his death to reminisce with me about his youth on Martha's Vineyard and sailing with his brother. I am particularly grateful also to Eleanor Lanahan, John's partner of 31 years, for generously sharing photographs she had gathered in an astonishing volume documenting John's life.

The work of transcribing these hours of conversation fell, thank God, to Sara Fogg Crafts, an esteemed newspaper colleague for many years. It wasn't easy work. Douglas mumbles, and through his mumbling blows a gale of seafaring expressions, unrecognizable to the uninitiated. Only the blessed and determined would stick it out. Sara did.

Betsy Corsiglia, also a longtime newspaper colleague, spent hours photographing Douglas's shoreside haunts and climbing over and around the jammed cement warehouse building that houses what Douglas calls his marine museum.

Thanks to Rob, Jamie, and Morgan Douglas, widely known as "the Douglas boys," a list which should include the fourth and youngest brother, Brooke, but he escaped despite my unholy pestering. Like so many who had spent time as *Shenandoah* crew, the brothers enthusiastically described the captain, but theirs was a particularly immeasurable contribution. Others could describe Douglas's leadership qualities, his devotion to his vessel, and his uncommon ways, but only his sons were describing the captain who was also their father.

Crewmembers Jerry Goodale, Tony Higgins, William Bunting, Dan Goodenough, John Mitchell, Gary Maynard, Bill Mabie, Scott Young, Matthew Stackpole, and others recalled their years of service as deckhands, bosuns, mates, and ultimately lifetime friends of Captain Douglas. Thanks too to Rick Perras, a college classmate of mine and a deckhand on *Shenandoah* in the late 1960s, now a retired lawyer, who generously agreed to read the first draft of the manuscript. Rick tackled the work in his meticulous, thoughtful way and offered encouragement, criticisms, and experience-based observations of Douglas, fortunately illuminating aspects of Douglas's character that seemed startlingly fresh in his memory after all these years and were often missed by others who fell victim to the lofty, perhaps aloof, view so many mistakenly attribute to *Shenandoah*'s master.

Thank you to Allan Miller, the builder of the Black Dog Tavern, for his help recalling its unusual and beloved beginnings and its part in the decade of ambitious and surprising change that added layers of business change to the Douglas/Shenandoah universe. And to Allan's partner Pamela Burke, thank you for discovering in an image of Douglas the latent figure of the polymath Benjamin Franklin.

Finally, thanks to Jonathan Eaton, co-publisher of Tilbury House Publishers, who has something of a seagoing pedigree himself, for his careful helmsmanship of this project and his vision, thoughtfulness, and patience. To his wife, Mariellen, a bold researcher of one of the deepest puzzles that challenged me, thank you for getting the tree thing right.

—DAC

Tributes

Captain Robert Douglas has been widely recognized for creating the topsail schooner *Shenandoah,* without question his life's centerpiece, and for his remarkably able, successful, and enduring 56-year career as her sole owner, manager, and master. Now 89 years old, Captain Douglas has been honored by fellow sailors and his Martha's Vineyard neighbors.

In February 2020, Tall Ships America bestowed on Captain Douglas its Lifetime Achievement Award, "given to an individual who has dedicated his or her life's work to getting people to sea under sail and has worked to preserve the traditions and skills of sail training." Two fellow mariners, Daniel Moreland and Gary Maynard, nominated Captain Douglas for the award.

Captain Daniel Moreland is a respected ship master and an internationally recognized authority on square-rigged and traditional sailing ships. He has circumnavigated the globe five times under sail, including four times in the barque *Picton Castle.* Captain Moreland's nomination remarks follow:

> Some time ago—never mind how long exactly—a young Air Force fighter pilot walked away from his downed and smoldering T-33. He paused to think again how he was living his life, and thought long and hard about living a different sort of life after that moment.
>
> He had in mind a life under sail, sharing the majesty of sailing ships and historic New England near his home on Martha's Vineyard. So, he set out to learn the craft of sail and to become a schooner captain.
>
> He succeeded beyond his imagination.

First, he headed to Maine and talked his way aboard some fine old schooners sailing the coast of Maine: legendary schooners like the *Alice S. Wentworth*, the *Stephen Taber*, the new-built *Mary Day*. Yet, he also wanted to learn something about square rigs for what he had in mind. So he signed aboard the solid and brand-new HMS *Bounty,* fitting out in Lunenburg, Nova Scotia, bound for Tahiti to make a movie. When he got back from the South Pacific, he set about designing his dream vessel. His sense of design is without peer.

Soon, oaken frames were going up at one of the last commercial wooden shipyards, the Harvey Gamage Shipyard in Maine. And in 1964 the Coastwise Packet Company took delivery of what would become the last wooden square-rigger to be built in these United States without auxiliary power.

Since that year—the same year the Beatles were welcomed to these shores—not a summer has gone by without the exquisite topsail schooner *Shenandoah* sailing the waters of southern New England with Captain Bob Douglas at the helm, and with a shipload of new seafarers soaking in a life you can only read about. Generations of young people have gotten their first taste of the salt sea, wood and canvas, burbling wake, and the teamwork required to sail such a vessel effectively on *Shenandoah*.

Adults, yes, they sailed as well, but kids, kids, kids. And pitching in with American Sail Training Association's first tall ship race along with *Tabor Boy, Bill of Rights, Brilliant*, and *Black Pearl*.

So many mariners got their start in *Shenandoah*. Masters, mates, riggers, tugboat skippers, model makers, boatbuilders, roofers, and also just good outstanding citizens.

And in so many ways, large and small and always quietly, Bob has given a boost to so many others to begin to live their dream under sail. The brigantine *Romance*; the historic schooners *Ernestina, Adventure, Ladona, Sylvina Beale, Alvei*, and the lovely *Violet*; and the barque *Picton Castle*. Even the old Gloucester fishing schooner *Evelina M. Goulart* made her way back up the Essex River to teach shipbuilding at her place of birth. That was all Bob.

From small craft to large, he has nudged and helped so many. The world of sail training is a vastly richer place for having Bob Douglas in it.

Did I mention kids? Every fifth-grade class on Martha's Vineyard has been able to sail for a week and tread the oiled pine decks of their own clipper schooner for the last few decades. Changing lives for the better every time.

And the island itself is all the better for the power of example of one man. Vineyard Haven is now a mecca for classic wooden sail. It could well have gone another way but for Bob Douglas. And then to top it off he rebuilt the 90-foot pilot schooner *Alabama* and took still more kids sailing.

At some point he came alongside his shipmate for life, a strong and beautiful lady he met in the venerable three-master *Victory Chimes*. Charlene has been his co-pilot and forward lookout for every sea mile together. Thank you, Charlene!

There may have been some kids somewhere—boyz, I think—a shout-out to Robbie, Jamie, Morgan, Brooke, and their growing families!

Captain Douglas, thank you for your service. Thank you for your devotion, making this a lifetime of achievement. Thank you for sharing your passion so readily and broadly. Thank you for your friendship.

And thanks for giving your precious *Shenandoah* to Ian and Casey to carry on your good works with their new organization, FUEL.

Gary Maynard, a former mate on *Shenandoah,* an ocean sailor, and a homebuilder on Martha's Vineyard, was the second mariner to propose Captain Douglas for the Tall Ships America award. Here are his remarks:

I am deeply grateful to be able to speak tonight and to honor my beloved friend, Captain Bob Douglas.

As Dan has shown, this remarkable sailor and shipowner has been an unequalled keeper of the flame in the final moments of the sunset of the Great Age of Sail, but more importantly, Bob Douglas has had a profound influence on hundreds of young men and women over a half-century in command of his magnificent *Shenandoah*. I will tell you my story, bearing in mind that it is only one story of many, many stories of lives this man has touched.

When I heard that Bob had given his schooner to FUEL, the news struck me deeply. You see, Harvey Gamage laid the keel of *Shenandoah* the year I was born, and *Shenandoah* has always been a presence in my life. I vividly remember her coming up Fishers Island Sound when I couldn't have been more than eight years old, a vast, looming apparition of spars and canvas and gleaming white topsides. As she glided past our little Key West smack, an imposing red-haired man leaned over the stern davits, watched for a few moments, and gave us a wave. Bob has always been a sucker for a pretty boat.

I signed aboard *Shenandoah* at sixteen, washed dishes, set tables, tended the coal stove, jumped through hoops for the mad cook, and set about learning the lines, the commands, the maneuvers, the routines, and the culture that would allow me to rise through the ranks from galley boy to deckhand to bosun and then mate. I learned to line up the cut cobalt glasses when setting the eighteen-foot mahogany tables, to black the stove, to clean the skylight so the mate couldn't wipe a finger around the lip and find coal dust. I learned to chamois varnish, polish brass, to jump for a bucket and sponge should a footprint appear on the paintwork. I learned to roll a topsail bunt so tight it couldn't be seen from the deck, to haul a brace with everything I could muster, to race aloft to handle sail, to pilot a yawl boat under the stern in a chop. I learned to sand and caulk and paint with no curtains, no holidays, and no splatter. I learned to herringbone a torn headsail, to trim a lamp wick to perfection. There were no lessons, no program, no instruction, no praise, only the highest of expectations. We sailed on and off the hook, spreading all canvas in minutes, everything on the double. Later in the day, we would roar into a familiar harbor all sail set, only to round-to and douse sail swiftly and without a hitch, and we would flake her great white wings for the night, the miter seams running precisely up the center of the stowed headsails where they sat high and tight on the top of the jibboom.

The magnificent vessel herself was only part of the tapestry being rewoven by the forbidding, quiet man with the flaming sideburns who stood all day, every day, year after year, back at the wheel. It was the traditions that Bob Douglas saw disappearing in the sunset, those threads of knowledge passed down since the dawn, those standards, those hard-earned rites of passage that made his working vessel so dynamic, so real, and so important.

My wife Kristi and I met and were married aboard *Shenandoah*. Kristi was herself once a Sunday bunk-maker on the schooner (ask her about the required ten inches of turndown, and yes, Bob does carry a tape measure). We bought our own *Violet* from Bob and rebuilt her in his shop at Five Corners. Bob, his lovely wife Charlene, and I continued working together for another fifteen years as I became a boat carpenter, a shipwright, a spar builder, a rigger, and a schooner captain, culminating in our resurrection of the 1926 McManus pilot schooner *Alabama*. In these efforts, and indeed in all things, I strived for the integrity and the excellence that I learned aboard *Shenandoah*.

I was given three minutes tonight to pay tribute to the life of a man who truly did what he was put on this watery planet to do, and who played so powerful a role in my own few years here. With regret, I will have to save the countless stories I could tell of this wonderful man for another gam in another anchorage.

I thanked Bob recently for allowing me to be a part of it all, to be the mate of a topsail schooner in the twentieth century, to sail and live and love her in the tradition of the great tea clippers. I told him *Shenandoah* was still my favorite vessel of all. His eyes lit up and he beamed and gave me a bear hug. In forty years, I had never told him this, and we had never hugged. This tribute, Bob, is my hug, our hug, in return.

Captain Douglas also received the Martha's Vineyard Community Foundation's Creative Living Award for 2020 – 2021. Here are the remarks delivered by Emily Bramhall, foundation director, in the 2021 ceremony:

Designed to honor the spirit of our initial donor Ruth Bogan and to recognize and celebrate "fine craftsmanship, creativity and ingenuity," this award recognizes Islanders for their efforts to "enhance and preserve the quality of life on the Vineyard forever."

And there is no doubt that Captain Robert Douglas has enhanced and preserved the quality of life on the Vineyard. Over many decades of dedication, passion, and hard work, Bob has embodied the very best of what this Island represents, sharing so generously his vision and life's work with the Island community, which in turn, has embraced it as its own.

The Vineyard Haven harbor that we know today, known worldwide as a wooden boat mecca, had its roots with the arrival in 1964 of Captain Douglas's *Shenandoah.* Her arrival ushered in an era of sailing and wooden boat building and appreciation that continues to this day.

The Creative Living Award has long been a celebration of the fabric of our community, and Bob Douglas is a strong and unique thread in that fabric.

Captain Douglas represents the very essence of this award—and beyond that, the essence of this community. He is hardworking, dedicated, independent, has great attention to authenticity and detail, is modest about his achievements and generous with his accomplishments. We have all benefited from his vision, be it as observers of the glorious collection of wooden schooners in our midst or as participants as crewmembers on his vessels.

And it must be noted that his wife Charlene has been a steadfast presence at his side, sharing in and passionately supporting his dedication to his vision. Just last week she and I were watching *Shenandoah* and *Lynx* rounding West Chop in a stiff southwest breeze, and she exclaimed with pride and affection about the beauty of the schooner, as if this were the first time she was seeing it. It was such a lovely example of the connection they share.

How fitting to be here tonight, in this beautiful setting on the shop floor of Gannon and Benjamin Marine Railway, at the edge of the harbor Bob has called home for over 60 years, among the boats and craftsmanship that he ushered in and the community he has inspired.